C000099191

With Unvei

Also by the same author:

Care in a Confused Climate

With Unveiled Face

A Pastoral and Theological Exploration of Shame

PAUL GOODLIFF

DARTON·LONGMAN+TODD

First published in 2005 by
Darton, Longman and Todd Ltd
1 Spencer Court
140–142 Wandsworth High Street
London
SW18 4JJ

ISBN 0 232 52574 9

A catalogue record for this book is available from the British Library.

Designed by Sandie Boccacci
Phototypeset in 10.5/13.75 Palatino by Intype Libra Ltd
Printed and bound in Great Britain by
Page Bros, Norwich, Norfolk

CONTENTS

ACKNOWLEDGEMENTS

THIS BOOK GREW out of an address I gave at a Swanwick Conference for Pastoral Care and Counsel, 'Continuing the Journey'. The planning groups for both that conference and the one that preceded it two years earlier were amongst the most honest and stimulating of groups that I have played a part in. At times focused on its work (and as chair, I hope I kept it sufficiently to task) but at other times deeply personal and pastoral, it was wonderfully fresh air to breathe. I owe a debt to those who served with me on the group.

The time taken to write the book was stolen from other commitments, and I want to acknowledge the gift of study leave taken while I was General Superintendent of the Central Area of the Baptist Union, and subsequently Regional Minister for the Central Baptist Association. My colleagues Stephen Copson, Helen Wordsworth and Colin Pye were unfailingly supportive, and the Moderator of the Association Council, Michael Bochenski, encouraged me to finish the book in the midst of all the challenges of establishing a new Regional Association. That I did not complete it until in my new post as Head of Ministry for the Baptist Union is no one's fault but mine. My colleagues at Baptist House have only lived with this for a brief period, but it would be ungracious not to acknowledge their support.

The real heroes, of course, are the men and women with whom it has been a privilege to journey in a counselling relationship as my clients. Confidentiality prevents me from naming and honouring them, but they know who they are, and my intention is that no one else will be able to identify them from reading parts of this book.

My dear friends Geoff Colmer and Alistair Ross have read some of the book in draft form, and their helpful comments have, I hope, improved it. Their companionship for many years has been one of the richest of experiences, and has contributed to this book in many unseen ways. The shortcomings remain mine. Successive editors at Darton, Longman and Todd have stuck with the project, and encouraged me, even when others far more gifted than I published books more profound than this at an early stage in the process and I was tempted to throw in the towel. Stephen Pattison's book on shame was published after I had written only a couple of chapters, and much that is best here is owed to my reading and benefiting from this magisterial study. Its influence will be felt in many sections.

The people who have paid the highest price in coping with my absence are my sons, Andrew, Nicholas and Stephen who are neither shameless, nor shame-filled, and I hope will always remain so, and Gill, my wife, friend, companion on life's journey, critical reader and greatest support, and of whom I am never ashamed! To them I owe the greatest debt of gratitude.

PREFACE

THE CHRISTIAN CHURCH has a long acquaintance with guilt, and some sections of the church might seem to be unhealthily obsessed with it, but shame is a more hidden matter: less attended to, but equally pervasive and just as damaging to individuals and communities alike. This book is an exploration of the causes, shapes and landscapes of shame, and offers a way in which unhealthy shame might be addressed and healed. The resources that I have turned to include the Scriptures, the insights of psychology and theology, and my experience in working pastorally with counselling clients who have been in the grip of chronic destructive shame.

MOSES HAD A PROBLEM. The appointment at the top of Mount Sinai had given his face an extraordinary appearance: it shone with a light that was like the radiance of God's glory.[1] Initially, Moses did not know this: after all, who can see his own face? But the cause of people's strange reluctance to come close soon became clear, and the strategy that Moses adopted was to cover his face with a veil. The only place where the veil was removed was in God's presence.

Some Jewish and Samaritan traditions held that this radiance did not fade until the day Moses died, but Paul, in his comments in 2 Corinthians 3 on this tradition, seems to favour a different version, whereby the glory gradually faded.[2] In Paul's estimation, the initial purpose of the veil – to protect the Israelites – soon became distorted and transformed into a protection for Moses' ego. He did not want the people to see that the radiance was fading. At the heart of this response is the experience of shame. In a later chapter I shall comment further on this central story about shame and Paul's use of it in 2 Corinthians 3 and 4, but here I want to observe, at the outset of this exploration about shame, that shame has both a protective and a destructive dimension.[3] What we might call protective shame, or discretion shame, is the way in which a proper sense of shame or discretion protects us from shameful behaviour. Associated with discretion shame is tact, respect for others and their values, sensitivity and an awareness of when our words or actions have stung another's self-esteem and self-worth. It is one of the constraints upon human desire that, unchecked, would bring harm. A man sees an attractive woman and his sex drive kicks in. Without, amongst other things, a proper sense of shame, he might pursue her, stalk her or even attack her. Thankfully, the sense of shame that most of us have protects both of them. Instead of exploiting others, shame helps us value them as people as opposed to thinking of them as objects to be used. So he admires briefly from a distance, brings his thoughts back under control and shame has saved him from harm. I am glad for that shame, in so many different experiences: it is not shameful to be influenced by this dimension of shame. Even in seemingly trivial exercises such as the choice of what I shall wear on a particular occasion, discretion shame is engaged. As I write this I am deliberating about what to wear to my parents' Golden Wedding celebrations tomorrow. What will honour such an occasion? A suit might be appropriate for the service in the church where they were married fifty years ago and where they will renew those marriage vows, particularly as I am reading a lesson. But later, at the more informal celebrations, might it seem too formal and distant? Certainly, despite the promise of a (rare) hot day in Sussex, I will not be wearing shorts and a t-shirt, for that would bring shame on me and on my parents, not to mention acute embarrassment to my three sons and my wife, Gill. My sense of wearing what is appropriate is informed by discretion shame, a sense which seemed to be entirely lacking when Elizabeth Hurley wore diamante-encrusted knickers to the wedding at which she was a guest, and stole the limelight from the bride, or when Raquel Welch's outfit outshone that of her daughter-in-law at the wedding of her son. These outfits, revealing altogether too much leg or *décolletage* at a formal public occasion, were derided for their lack of taste. What you wear on the beach and in church are different because of this social control of discretion shame. The Talmud says 'A sense of shame is a lovely sign in a man. Whoever has a sense of shame will not sin so quickly; but whoever shows no sense of shame in his visage, his father surely never stood on Mount Sinai.'[4]

Stephanie Dowrick puts it like this:

> Restraint offers a space between intention and action and the opportunity to protect others from actions or reactions that should exist only in your imagination. The more conscious you are of that space, and the freer you are to occupy it, the more easily you can choose whether and how to act.[5]

Discretion shame is one of the powers that shape restraint. To live otherwise makes me 'shameless', lacking a proper dimension of protective shame. The 'shameless' engage in 'shameful' actions, and in some cultures the punishment is public 'shaming'.

There is, however, another dimension to shame. It is fragile and can easily be twisted into a destructive condition that imprisons a person, controlling their ability to be true to themselves and preventing the vulnerability and openness in people that is essential in deep human relationships. This touches on our true identity as children of God, made in his image. It distorts the heart and soul, and wants to hide. Like Moses hiding his shame behind a veil, the person experiencing acute shame wants to hide away, or at least to hide their face. In many cultures, a sense of shame is accompanied by covering the face with the hands. The sufferer from this acute shame wants to 'fall through the floor', says 'I wish the ground would open up and swallow me whole', and wants to cease to be, to cease to exist. This acute shame, if it becomes chronic, can lead to self-destructive behaviours, self-harming and even suicide.

Alison grew up dominated by a manipulative mother who seems to have resented her and who controlled her emotionally and sexually. She remembers the image of her mother's face as hard or blank, unsmiling. Alison's sense of worth was always low, and she could never remember valuing herself or her opinions as a child. Her adult experience was one of self-loathing and guilt and, essentially, shame. When she was overwhelmed by these feelings she cut her arms with a razor, or hid in a darkened room with symptoms that are similar to clinical depression. She approached a counsellor when suicide became a very real option, yet she wanted to live. Shame had led to an inner fragmentation and pursuit of self-destruction.

In trying to deal with such conflicting emotions, an awkward space opens up within us: the soul becomes divided. In extreme instances, such inner division can result in dissociative disorders. A variant upon it is a flight to utterly shameless actions (the response of the sociopath) or a destructive narcissism; a desire to control the inner painful turmoil by controlling the world outside by power, force or money.

One of the most challenging and painful aspects of my previous role in ministry, offering oversight to Baptist churches and their clergy as a Regional Minister (the closest Baptists get to translocal *episcope*), and in my current role, responsible for all ministry matters for the Baptist Union, is working with churches where their pastor has been exposed after engaging in an adulterous affair over a number of months or years. Thankfully this is rare, but when it does happen, not only is the minister filled with shame, it overflows to his family and his congregation, who feel betrayed and angry that one whom they trusted implicitly has shown himself to have acted without proper restraint. The whole church is affected by the sense of shame, while only the minister is guilty. Shame is a 'sticky' emotion, and spreads like syrup from a broken jar on the kitchen floor. The disgrace shame sticks to himself, his wife, his children, his church and, to a lesser degree, to his profession. It is different to guilt (which one hopes the disgraced minister also feels), for it is felt by the innocent. The betrayed wife is certainly not guilty, but she feels the shame acutely.

4

In summary, Fowler says,

Shame is related to the deepest places of truth in our souls. Shame cuts to the heart. In its healthy forms it helps to form and inform the heart. Shame provides a primary foundation for the conscience, and for the instinctive sense of what is worthy or unworthy, right or wrong. Shame, as an emotion, relates to the sensitive feelings touched in love and deep communion with others. Shame protects the intimacy of our closest relations with friends, lovers, spouses or children. It surrounds our relation with the Holy or the domain of what is sacred to us. Shame, in its positive influence, is the caretaker of our worthy selves and identities. When we listen attentively to the voice of our healthy shame, we speak and act from our 'centre'. Shame has a special role to play in matters attending to the spirit and in the care and nurture of the soul.

In its distorted forms, however, shame can misshape or 'break' the heart. It can cut off sensitive access to the places of truth and transcendence in our own hearts. It can lead us to create 'false selves' in order to meet the conditions of worth in our families of origin, or in our workplaces, social roles, or even in our churches or synagogues. Shame distorts our relations whenever power discrepancies based upon class, gender, race, sexual orientation, or religious commitments become established and taken for granted. In its most distorted forms, excessive shame can lead to the 'shameless' orientations of sociopaths or to the super-narcissism we see embodied in some political dictators, money magnates, and celebrities in our world.[6]

This book is an exploration of shame in both its variants. I will argue that we need to reinforce the protective purpose of shame, for that ultimately serves the purposes of a good society, but find ways of healing destructive shame.

To engage in the latter we need to understand some of its roots, and part of this exploration will engage with the psychology and origins of destructive shame in early childhood.[7] We shall also need to view its current manifestations in the twenty-first century. One perspective on shame is that we live in a narcissistic culture,[8] and that destructive shame has assumed epidemic proportions as a malady of the soul. We shall also want to explore the cure for destructive shame and that will engage us in theology and spirituality.

Unless we identify and work with this elusive and shy emotion, seek to bring healing from its toxic effects and create communities that do not exploit shame for purposes of power and control, we shall be condemned to remain in a culture of spiritual deadness and chronic emotional pain. A culture that can deal more graciously with shame, however, is empowered to 'face the social and economic injustices of our common lives. This comes from our own "good-enoughness" – a sufficiency based on our true worth – and in our effective power to make this a better world.'[9]

We must differentiate shame from guilt, for they appear, superficially, to be similar. Noting that they are commonly confused, Schneider remarks 'Shame and guilt are linked like ham and eggs.'[10] The shame family of experiences includes embarrassment, humiliation, disgrace, shyness, modesty, pride, ridicule and narcissism. The family of emotions linked to guilt is different and includes injury, duty, offence, transgression, culpability, wrong and good/bad. Guilt does not always require an object: I might just feel guilty, if this affect has been inured in the soul through repressive parenting, whereas I am always ashamed of something and this involves the whole self. I might be ashamed of my size, my accent, my upbringing or my taste, but I am never just ashamed. Shame about a particular facet of my life touches my whole self and affects how I think about myself.

Guilt is concerned with what I have done wrong, and its cure is reparation and forgiveness. If by my actions I am guilty of harming someone, I might feel the wretchedness of guilt, but I can do something about it, and that involves disclosure. Shame is more stubborn, and concerns who I am, not what I have done. Shame is not cured by disclosure or by confession, for it craves concealment, hiddenness and flight. It is an altogether more profound and disturbing emotion, yet too often the church has centred on guilt and pardon. Perhaps guilt is easier to 'cure', seems closer to the biblical message about forgiveness or is simply less problematic. The church knows a great deal about guilt, but little about shame. It is high time that was changed.

In fact, the psychological world has only recently begun to take sufficient notice of shame. Speaking at a Clinical Theology Association conference in 1996, Professor John Patton describes how, when, fifteen years ago, he first began to research shame he looked in vain in the psychological dictionaries. It was not dealt with as a separate entry, but was accessed through the rubric 'guilt'. He continues with reference to the Philadelphia psychiatrist Donald Nathanson, who describes his sense of inadequacy that he did not know very much about the affect shame. In twenty years of psychiatric practice, he says, he had had no training that dealt with shame or the shame family of emotions. No one in a case conference had ever talked about shame, or recommended a reference to it. He believes that a great many of his unsuccessful cases related to his failure to identify shame. 'Whatever we had not understood turned out to be shame.'[11] In my own experience as a minister and pastoral counsellor, it seems that shame has played a greater role in the destruction of my clients' mental health than has guilt, although there are some members of the Christian communities that I have served whose main struggle is with an overwhelming sense of guilt.

Before I outline what this book will explore, I would like to add a word of explanation about the clinical material included. In order to protect the confidentiality of those counselling clients with whom I have worked over the years, not only have I changed names, but also the material facts. No doubt, clients or former clients might hear echoes of their own stories in the clinical material included, but I hope that no one will identify an individual from the details given, and if they think they do, they will almost certainly be mistaken!

So, to the structure of this pastoral and theological exploration.

We shall begin with a review of the stories from Scripture and ancient myth that seek to explain the phenomenon of shame. From the story of the Fall in Genesis to the myth of Narcissus, from the parable of the Prodigal Son in Luke 15 and the story of the sinful woman in Luke 7 to St Paul's observations about the face of Christ in 2 Corinthians 4, we shall see that the affect 'shame' has been one of central concern in biblical and ancient literature.

With the myth of Narcissus in particular, I shall identify the condition of narcissistic disturbance and the psychology of acute and chronic shame. The illness formerly called 'multiple personality disorder', now properly called 'dissociative identity disorder', has a particular relationship with shame, and we shall look in some detail at this condition, in both its extreme manifestations and its more subtle, less severe forms.

This will require a closer look at the origins of shame. From a theological perspective I shall argue that it has some of its roots in cosmic dread, the experience of the presence of the divine that fills us with either dread or awe. From the psychological perspective, its origins in the infant–mother relationship are especially important. The standard psychoanalytical approach sees both shame and guilt as the result of tensions between the ego and superego, with shame being the consequence of failure and shortcomings. That observation relies upon the belief that the psyche is structured in classical psychoanalytical ways, of course. Knowing shame's proper function will help us understand why it sometimes 'goes wrong' and becomes a distorted and destructive power in a person's life.

In the central section we shall use the metaphor of the face as a bridge from the first half of the book, which seeks to understand the condition, to the second half, which will point towards ways of healing the destructive dimensions of shame in pastoral care and counselling. The face is a central metaphor because in some ways shame is most clearly expressed through the expression on the face and the hands, which come together as the shamed person covers their face with their hands.[12] The etymological root of the word 'shame' from the Indo-European family of languages (*kam/kem*) means 'to cover'. The idea of being covered up to avoid shame is widespread. We speak of 'bowing the head in shame' or its converse, walking 'head held high' by those unencumbered by shame. Many psychotherapists consider the gaze of the infant at its mother's face to be of considerable importance in developing or failing to develop a healthy sense of trust and shame. In 2 Corinthians Paul speaks of the glory of God seen in the face of Christ, and I shall argue that one starting point for healing excessive shame is the contemplation of the face of Christ, both metaphorically and, through the medium of the icon, in some ways in actuality. It is in relationship to the gracious acceptance of Christ, taking us as we are, that a fundamental healing begins. But it does not stop there.

The healing of shame comes from acceptance of who we are, and in the pastoral life of the church that is expressed in Eucharist and fellowship. The pastoral task here is to allow such dimensions of community to develop that we are able to give expression to our deepest longings and fears without rejection by others, or such acute embarrassment and shame that we turn away. Prayer is one way of expressing the emotions in those deep places, praise another, and a tender embrace another. There is a longing for churches where prayer can be poured out, praise offered in extravagance and love shared that does not abuse the other, or reinforce shame. The pastoral leader has a special responsibility to foster such communities, in the hope that the Christian church might point to a better way of living than is common in the shame-lessness and shame-filled-ness of postmodern culture.

CHAPTER 1

> ✦

The Experience of Shame

IN THESE OPENING chapters I want to investigate a number of facets of the experience of shame, using sources ranging from Greek mythology to contemporary psychotherapy and from clinical experience to cultural studies. Since the roots of the Christian faith are in the experience of a particular ancient Near-Eastern culture, I would like to begin with the biblical tradition, both in the Old and New Testaments.

The ancient cultures of the Near-East, including that of Israel before Christ and the Jewish culture in which he lived, were acutely aware of the power of shame as a personal experience and as a force of social control. Generally, shame in the Old Testament is an experience of corporate humiliation. The Psalmist speaks of the way in which Yahweh will humiliate the evil-doer, putting them to shame (Pss 40:14; 83:16–18) and Prophet and Psalmist alike pray that the ungodly will be put to shame (Pss 6:10; 35:26; Isa. 1:29; Jer. 2:26). Correspondingly, in his prayer for deliverance from persecution, David prays

> Do not let those who hope in you be put to shame
>> because of me,
>>> O Lord God of Hosts;
> do not let those who seek you be dishonoured because
>> of me,
>>> O God of Israel.
> It is for your sake that I have borne reproach,
>> that shame has covered my face.
>
> (Psalm 69:6–7)

The shame that 'covers his face' is expressed by the hiding of the face behind hand or veil.

The translators of the Old Testament texts into Greek, the writers of the Septuagint, use the Greek verb αισχυνω (*aischyno*) for the Hebrew *bos*, 'to put to shame', and the noun αισχυνη (*aischyne*) for the Hebrew nouns *bos*, *busah* or *boset*. These meanings predominate, although on eight occasions the noun *aischyne* is employed to translate *erwah*, meaning the pudenda or genitals (note, pudenda from the Latin *pudeo*, to be ashamed). The link between sex and shame is ancient. The same Greek word, *aischyno*, is used in the normative passage of Genesis 2:25, 'They were naked and not ashamed.' The absence of shame is contrasted with its presence after the disobedience of the eating of the fruit of the forbidden tree. Afterwards, their eyes are opened to their nakedness, and they sew fig leaves for loin cloths and hide in the Garden. Their genitals, symbol of physical sexuality, which had remained visible, are now a cause of shame, or if we were to use the word adopted by the Septuagint translators, *aischyne*, it is literally 'their shame'. The New Testament shares the same language as the Septuagint, but the word group *aischyne* is found much less frequently. Of the Gospel writers, only Mark and Luke use *epaischynomai*, 'be ashamed', where the word means being ashamed of confessing Christ, or afraid of human ridicule.

Fowler, following the psychotherapist Eric Erikson, sees in this the second creation story in Genesis, which tells not only of the creation of humankind, but of our fall from innocence, a memory, collective as well as personal, of that time of responsive care, milk flowing from the breast, and loving eyes that mark our pre-weaning utopias. In place of the self-unaware, unreflective bliss of the first six months of our existence comes the beginnings of those parental parameters for our growth and safety against which we kick: mother's milk is replaced by solid food and the pain of teething signals the approaching end of our gummy sucking on the nipple.

Instead of everything we could possibly do being permissible, our growing abilities and mobility demand limits and prohibitions. The all-accepting parent now signals disapproval, and before long our own self-awareness will make others strange. Soon, shame will be a possibility.

In the Genesis account, shame, absent from the experience until the fruit of knowledge is tasted, becomes dominant. There comes a painful awareness of nakedness: eyes are averted, heads downcast, coverings are fashioned. Adam and Eve's awareness of shame results in their hiding from God, and his judgement upon their action is expulsion from the Garden, and its resultant alienation from him, from each other, and from the created order. Michelangelo, in his mighty Sistine Chapel ceiling (1508–12), depicts the Expulsion with powerful precision. Adam is unrepentant, his outstretched arms rejecting the edict which expels them from the Garden. Eve hides behind her husband's rather bulky body (muscle tone turning to middle-age spread!), concealing her breasts behind her crossed forearms, but with a look of sheer hatred upon her face. Michelangelo relied heavily for the structure of this panel upon the earlier Expulsion, that painted eighty years earlier by Masaccio between 1427 and 1428, found in the Cappella Brancacci, in Santa Maria del Carmine in Florence and reproduced on the cover of this book. Here, with greater emotional force, a leaner pair are expelled from the Garden. Both naked, Adam covers his bowed face with his hands, full of shame, while Eve, one hand covering her breasts, the other her genitals, cries out in despair and horror at the prospect of living in the bare landscape which faces them outside the gates of Paradise. It is Masaccio who has captured correctly the shame and terror of this judgement, his pair broken in spirit, where Michelangelo's remain defiant.[1] Raphael follows the Masaccio depiction, with Adam's bowed and covered face, in the painting by one of his pupils, following the master's design, found

13

in the *Loggie di Rafaello* in the Vatican, but the overall effect is less powerful.[2]

Fowler comments that as a child collides with the structures of limits, demands, expectations and disciplines, and with the reality that he or she faces competition with others for attention and objects, so he or she will have murderous thoughts towards siblings and parents – thoughts given expression in the next story in Genesis, that of Cain and the murder of Abel:

> To bring insights on the dynamics of shame into the interpretation of the Genesis 3 story of Eve, Adam, and 'the Fall' is to see our kinship with our forebears in new ways. To couch the story in terms of the issues of 'autonomy versus shame and doubt' rather than those of 'initiative versus guilt' (Erikson) places the encounter with the serpent, the forbidden fruit, and the awakening to nakedness and shame in a different frame. It alters the meaning of disobedience and changes the valency of any charge of excessive pride.[3]

Paul uses the language of shame in a forensic sense, not a psychological one. So, in Romans 1:16, 'I am not ashamed of the Gospel' means 'I am willing to confess the Gospel.' To the cultures of his day, the gospel seemed rooted in an event of utter shamefulness: the public execution of a common criminal by the means reserved for slaves and rebels, crucifixion. The early Christians, Paul included, were identifying themselves with this shaming event, yet found that it carried, for them, no shame. On the contrary, Paul would not use the 'lofty words' of rhetoric or wisdom, but simply proclaim 'Christ, and him crucified' (1 Cor. 2:2). In the cross of Christ, these early Christians had found the power of public shame turned to intense pride.

In his missionary work, the Apostle does not want to work in vain, and in 2 Corinthians 7:14 and 9:4 he uses the word *kataischyno*, 'I was not ashamed', to mean that the qualities of

14

the Corinthian church about which Paul had boasted to Titus had been proved accurate. He was not embarrassed by them. This has little to do with the experience of shame about which this study is concerned.

The noun *aischyne,* shame, is used by Jude of those false teachers troubling the church, who seem to be advocating a libertine lifestyle, and where shame is linked to sexual sin, and the same word is employed by Paul in 2 Corinthians 4:2 to refer to disgraceful and underhand ways of manipulating others, and in Philippians 3:19 to refer to the carnal (and sexual) attitudes and practices of those who 'live as enemies of the cross of Christ.' In Hebrews 12:2, Jesus Christ is described as 'despising the shame' of the public humiliation of death as a common criminal, which gets closer to the psychological experience of shame which we are concerned to explore. All in all the use of the word 'shame' in the New Testament testifies more to the cultural controls of shaming than to a personal experience of feelings of shame. To explore the experience of shame in the New Testament we would do better to consider the ways in which Jesus relates to those consumed by shame, and this we will do in another chapter.

Shame is something which the Israelite would wish upon his enemy and want to avoid himself, and so it becomes a powerful tool of social control. Stockitt[4] uses the illustration from Deuteronomy 25:5–10, where the brother who fails to perform his duty towards his brother's widow by giving her children and thus carrying on the family line is publicly shamed in the presence of the elders by the woman who takes off one of his sandals and spits in his face, saying 'This is what is done to the man who will not build up his brother's family line.' Henceforth that man's family would be known as 'Unsandalled'. The brother who had rejected and shamed his sister-in-law was thus shamed by the whole community. The beauty of the story of Ruth is precisely in how a shamed woman is honoured by Boaz as he acts as the kinsman-redeemer (*levir*), who takes her as his wife and thus removes her shame from her. His action was so that 'all the assembly of my people may know that you are a worthy woman' (Ruth 3:11). Unlike the shaming by the rejected woman in Deuteronomy 25, in Ruth the sandal is exchanged as a sign of the legitimacy of the transaction, as a nearer relative forgoes his right to act as *levir* in favour of the older and more distant kinsman, Boaz, who has no doubt fallen in love with the young Moabite woman.[5]

In common with many more primitive cultures, where honour is a valuable commodity, shame is used as a means of control: the fear of public shaming acting as a powerful deterrent against anti-social behaviour. This can seem quite alien to our culture in twenty-first-century liberal Britain. In 1999 a suggestion that those whom the courts sentenced to community service as an alternative to a custodial sentence should wear distinctive dress while performing that service was roundly condemned as too humiliating and shaming: a step too far. Other cultures might consider the current social anonymity afforded to those on community service not sufficiently shaming to act as a deterrent to others. In a subsequent chapter we shall look at the ways in which shame, like much else, has become privatised in postmodern culture, but here, just note how alien the notion of 'public shaming' has become. Precisely because it is not regulated in social codes, public shame becomes more difficult to anticipate. Young men, for instance, consider the expression of emotions such as sadness, anxiety or despair shameful, especially if accompanied by weeping. An unwritten code of peer group shaming prevents them from seeking help or expressing those emotions in a predominantly 'macho' culture, and one result is the high rate of suicide amongst young men in Britain.

CHAPTER 2

Jane's Story

IN ORDER FOR us to enter into the world of experience for those who are consumed with shame, I want to begin to tell you a story. It is a true story, inasmuch as it rings true for me as I have worked with counselling clients over the years, and draws upon their stories. However, it is not an account of any one particular client's story, as it would be improper to breach the confidentiality of the counselling relationship. And so here is the fictional story of Jane.

By the time Jane arrived seeking counselling she had been deeply depressed for some time and had begun self-harming. To some old white scars on her forearms had been added some red, raw new ones. Jane was a single woman, aged 32, holding down, barely, her job as a solicitor handling conveyancing and probate work in a local family firm of lawyers. It was becoming clear that she would soon no longer be able to hold things together sufficiently to continue in work without some support and help, and it was this fear of losing her job that drove her to her GP, who prescribed antidepressants and advised she seek counselling. Jane had become a Christian at university and continued to practise her faith throughout the struggles of her twenties and early thirties, but her church disapproved of secular approaches to mental health problems, and the most that Jane could risk (without alienating the pastoral support which she had hitherto relied upon) was help from a Christian counsellor.

Initially Jane sought help from her counsellor in order to cope with the pressures of work, but very soon it became apparent that the problems were not confined to stress at work, nor did they arise from there, but that their origins lay much deeper and further back in her past.

Jane had two siblings: a brother, Adam, seven years older, who was quick, bright, inordinately clever and adored by his parents and Jane alike, and a sister, Emily, four years older than Jane, and a rebel. What Emily lacked in academic brilliance she made up for in striking good looks and sporting flair. Jane felt she lacked both the sets of qualities of her older siblings, and considered herself rather slow at school, a plodder rather than a high flier, and hopeless at games. She lacked Emily's blonde hair and trim figure, and at the age of ten was acutely aware of her own shock of red hair and childish plumpness compared to Emily's adolescent figure, recently aided by a growth spurt in height without the gawkiness that had afflicted her older brother.

Adam always felt remote to Jane, not surprisingly since he generally ignored her. Jane's parents had protected Adam from the intrusions of his younger sisters by giving him his own room and warning them that he was not to be disturbed. Similar warnings often surrounded Jane's father, a barrister with a busy criminal practice, often home late and then with briefs to read and cases to prepare for. It was Jane's mother whose rage she feared if she disturbed the tranquillity of the household and it seemed to Jane that in the eyes of her mother every other member of the family counted for more than Jane. Indeed, it seemed as if at most times Jane was little more than a nuisance and an inconvenience, not so much an after-thought as a mistake. Jane's mother had later told her as much, in the heat of one angry exchange, when Jane was 21: 'You weren't planned, my girl. I hated every moment of carrying you and you've been a bloody nuisance ever since.'

Of course, Jane had known that throughout her childhood. She could barely remember any physical affection from her mother, although in company her mother might make a fuss of her. Her father was more affectionate, but mostly just wasn't there often enough. After her eighth birthday he wasn't there at all. The divorce between Jane's parents was financially civilised and emotionally messy. Jane's mother, Adam, Emily and Jane did not have to move house and Adam continued as a day pupil at the local minor public school. Emily attended the girl's grammar school nearby, where in time Jane would follow her, and the most profound change, it seemed to Jane, was not her father's absence (he had hardly been present for the eighteen months prior to his leaving home) but her mother's defiant search for work, picking up the pieces of the career in medicine that had been postponed by her falling pregnant with Jane nine years earlier. The break had been too long to make the grade she had longed for in paediatric medicine, and she had to settle, resentfully, for a senior house job rather than the consultant's post she might, or registrar's post she certainly would, have obtained.

In addition to this background of the absence of love, indeed the presence of resentment that often overflowed into emotional abuse on the part of her mother, in the course of counselling a story of some unusual sexual abuse emerged. Jane remembered occasions when her sister Emily, as a young adolescent, made unwanted sexual advances towards her, both in the bedroom they shared and elsewhere in the house. In due course Emily's sexuality took shape as a same-sex orientation, and these early experiments clearly presaged the settled lesbian relationships of her adult life, but for Jane, who remained heterosexual, they were disturbing and shameful experiences. She never tried to tell her mother, whom she was sure would not believe her, and carried these shame-filled memories as an enduring legacy of her own pre-adolescence.

Perhaps more disturbing were half-remembered fears of molestation from much earlier childhood (aged five or six), although the perpetrator remained unclear. Her mother's brother stayed often with the family throughout Jane's child-hood years, but the fears could equally have their origins

19

with Jane's father. With a highly charged sexuality and great charm, he had affairs on and off from long before Jane was born, and his unfaithfulness to Jane's mother was the prime cause of the breakdown of the marriage, but the question of whether he was also guilty of some sexual abuse of Jane (or Emily) remained in Jane's mind conjecture, albeit conjecture that haunted her. It was as if she did not want to accept the awful truth that he might have betrayed her in such a destructive way. Throughout her teenage years, Jane placed her father on an almost unassailable pedestal, completely splitting off the anger she also felt at his leaving the family. That anger Jane directed at her mother, and it was expressed in the simmering rows that would last for days.

Despite her sense of failure at her studies compared with Adam, Jane in her own steady way achieved a standard that enabled her to read law at a northern university. In her first year she had a flat-mate in halls who was an Evangelical Christian and a member of the Christian Union. Sandra took Jane to CU events and it was not long before she made a commitment to Christ. This conversion experience made relatively little impact upon the deeper levels of damage to her personality. Indeed, in large part, it was a desire to be accepted that had made this discovery of religion so easy, and it was not so much an acceptance by a loving God that had gripped her as the friendships she made with others in the CU. The church she attended with others from the halls on the outskirts of the city was of a kind that strongly preached conversion from sin, and in a way, it reinforced the sense of guilt and shame she carried. To be told that she was a miserable sinner week after week did nothing to alleviate her shame. It just reinforced her growing sense of alienation from God. In her head she knew that God loved everybody, but in her heart she was convinced that did not include her.

In her second year she fell deeply in love with a fellow law student in her class. The attraction to Robert was reciprocated, but he was not a Christian. True, he would go along with her to church from time to time, but it was clear that he had no desire to share her faith, and he had the personal integrity not to pretend to convert in order to keep her. The pressure from the Christian Union, and from her church's minister, to break off the relationship was steady. Over the Christmas of her third year she broke off the relationship with Robert, but not before they had been sleeping together for some weeks. This remained her secret, although she suspected some of her friends at CU knew. The guilt was intense, and the shame at her moral failure (exacerbated by her knowledge that her father and mother had parted because of his adultery) was acute for a while before it was buried under the pressures of finals, the search for a job and then the work as she took her articles.

The first job she had was in the south of England, and so she never returned to her family home to live. After a few years she moved on to the practice where she was working when the first signs of an approaching breakdown prompted her to seek counselling. She had maintained her Christian faith throughout those years, in both places attending strongly Evangelical churches, although remaining on the edge of their communities. Although accepted by many within those churches, she found it hard to commit herself to full participation. It was the pressure of work and living as a single woman, she told herself, but there was something else that niggled. Call it a reluctance to become too involved, perhaps, or a fear of rejection by others if they got to know her too well. The depth of her own self-loathing and disgust bubbled away beneath the surface, locked away from even her own self-reflective gaze, until the events that were to disturb that uneasy equilibrium.

The death of her father from a heart attack when she was 29 came as a complete surprise. He was only 61, she told herself, still practising at the bar. In fact he had been taken ill while in court, but was pronounced dead shortly after he arrived at the hospital. Jane had kept in touch with him, and

21

he had shown much greater interest in her after her legal career had begun. Indeed there were times when she almost felt close to him, although it tended to be she who travelled to see him rather than the other way round. True, there were occasions when a case he was prosecuting was held at the local Crown Court, and they almost always had dinner together. He never stayed with her, but then sleeping on a sofa-bed was not quite his style, and expenses always paid for a decent hotel room.

She heard about his death while working late the same afternoon that he had collapsed. It was Adam who phoned her and broke the news. Some corner of her defences was shattered with that news, and grief and guilt deepened into depression.

Jane always presented herself in black. A black suit and white shirt was the legal uniform at work, and she just continued it into her spare time. Black jeans or leggings and a large long-sleeved top or polo-neck jumper covered her body. It meant she could hide the scars on her arms and make herself invisible. She hated exposure and would never wear clothes that might flatter her figure. She had long lost the childhood plumpness which had caused her such distress when she compared herself with Emily, but her body was never a cause of delight or pride to Jane. Better to cover it up and have done with it.

In her journey with a counselling companion, Jane became aware of her anger towards her father and more aware of her feelings of guilt. In the early stages, however, she was unaware of her shame. It was as if it hid behind anger and grief, safer emotions to own up to. Her self was so fragile and fractured that shame was too dangerous a feeling, too all-encompassing. Even as the shame itself prompted her to hide her true self lest it be rejected (as it surely must, she felt), and to hide her body beneath dark shapeless layers, the shame hid away behind other members in the family of emotions: fear, guilt and anger.

What she did know were acute feelings of worthlessness and guilt. The guilt was not simply about words spoken by her which she now regretted, or actions worthy of rebuke. She knew about those feelings of guilt and could engage with her Christian teaching about confession and forgiveness, with some success in finding absolution for some sins committed. What always remained, however, was a mass of unattributable guilt: formless, unfocused, sour and heavy like winter clay. 'Guilt' was the word she used, but shame might be a more accurate description for this weight within her. It was not about the things she had said or done, or even thought, but about who she felt she was: a worse than worthless, bad person, to be summarily rejected and thrown out with the rubbish.

This shame was chronic and unresponsive to the prayers of others and the usual processes by which the church seeks to build up its members and enable them to grow in humanity, wholeness and faith. Nor was this unresponsiveness due primarily to a particularly twisted kind of faith taught in the churches she gravitated towards, a faith that knew a great deal about sin and guilt, but next to nothing about shame, and which through its ignorance and judgementalism nurtured shame rather than healed it. The shame she felt had not been produced by the church, although it had, perhaps, been exacerbated by the excessive emphasis upon the worthlessness of humanity without God. It had been there since before she could remember.

For the moment, we will leave Jane's story here and turn to some of the ways in which shame has been understood.

CHAPTER 3

The Origins of Shame

IF WE ARE to find appropriate and effective ways to alleviate chronic and destructive shame we first need to understand where it comes from and how it originates. However, there is no consensus about the origins of shame, with differing disciplines and psychological approaches offering differing theories. One of the difficulties in describing shame and discussing its origins is that by its very nature it wants to hide, to remain unspoken and inarticulate. Certainly, some find it hard to talk about their feelings of shame, not just because of the discomfort in doing so, but also because the experience is hard to put into words. In the counselling relationship, clients may find it easier to create visual images, or use metaphor and image, rather than articulate precise emotions.

In the Western religious traditions shame is viewed as an emotion associated with (or consequent to) guilt, and perhaps this assimilation of shame into the discussion of guilt in the wider culture is one reason why the psychoanalytic tradition in psychology paid scant regard to shame until quite recently. However, this tradition places the origins of shame in the earliest stages of human development, although there is confusion over the exact cause. The complex and disputed ideas of psychoanalytic theory need not concern us in this discussion.

Psychotherapeutic Approaches to Shame

Shame is one of the limited number of neurophysiological affects with which we are born, and an important approach to the origins of shame focuses upon the role played by adults, and especially parents, in creating shame responses in the developing child. Nathanson dedicates *Shame and Pride*[1] to Silvan Tomkins, whose affect theory of emotion has been influential on many psychologists of shame. Tomkins argued that there is a limited set of emotions that are triggered by stimuli at a basic biological level. These responses are short-lived, lasting a few seconds at most, but are common to everyone. Thus we can all recognise the affect anger because we have all experienced its powerful biological effect, although the reason for that trigger will be unique to every event. What makes me angry is down to my upbringing, the way my culture socialises anger and the injustices or losses that trigger anger in my own world, but the fact that we get angry is something which we share in our biological make-up. While the affect, the triggered response, lasts a moment, the emotion it gives rise to can be sustained over much longer periods of time. I can dwell on those causes of my anger, nurture the feelings, remember the other times I responded to injustice and become an angry person. Sometimes the prolonged emotion becomes a mood that is impossible to shift, particularly if one trigger is overlaid by others, or if triggers come in swift succession.

There are times when a mood simply won't go away, when nothing we can do will disperse it. In times like these we try everything, from the distraction or diversion offered by an entertainment or a holiday to a major reorganisation of life, such as a shift in career. Often such a mood will precipitate a person into psychotherapy.[2]

Tomkins divides the affect system into nine affects, three positive and six negative. In babies each affect has its characteristic facial expression, for instance the quivering lips of distress breaking into tears, or the wide-open mouth and eyes of surprise. The biological response to shame and humiliation is eyes averted, shoulders slumped and blushing. It is a response that results from the inner tensions provoked by a mismatch between the stimulus and the meaning given to it. Tomkins puts it thus:

> If distress is the affect of suffering, shame is the affect of indignity, of transgression and alienation. Though terror speaks to life and death and distress makes of the world a vale of tears, yet shame strikes deepest into the heart of man. While terror and distress hurt, they are wounds inflicted from outside which penetrate the smooth surface of the ego; but shame is felt as an inner torment, a sickness of the soul.[3]

Nathanson believes that guilt is a combination of shame and fear, the two affects fused and hooked together with a wide range of memories of situations in which we were caught doing forbidden things. Shame as an affect is a brief response, but it can be built into a major character trait, dominating a person's life, as the cumulative experiences of shame are remembered as 'scenes' to be replayed, with 'scripts' that are retold. Such chronic shame is allied to the narcissism explored by Kohut[4] and Mollon.[5]

In his discussion of the narcissistic personality, Mollon explores its affects and describes how shame has a great deal to do with the look and being looked at, with sexuality and with the body. The story of Narcissus echoes all these themes. The normal self-awareness can be distorted into a painful and embarrassed self-consciousness when a child is not recognised for who she really is, but becomes the object of her mother's desire to shape and control. 'The father does not intervene in such a way as to break this spell and allow the child her own identity. As a result, the child becomes prone to embarrassed self-consciousness in the discrepancy between who she is experienced to be.'[6]

Such embarrassed self-consciousness can become narcissistic vulnerability, a sensitivity to slights or being overlooked or treated disrespectfully, because the self is too fragile. The person has failed to evoke a thoughtful empathic response from parents. Instead of the mother's face expressing love and care, joy and concern, there is an awful blankness, a failure in mirroring which renders the child uncertain and mistrustful. The person reacts with rage or depression as well as shame. In reaction to that sense of humiliation arising from the narcissistic injuries to the self, there can be a defensive retreat into self-sufficiency and feelings of omni-competence.

The origins of narcissism, according to some psychoanalytical models (Klein in particular), lie in the compensation of the child's fears and anxieties with fantasies of wealth, beauty and omnipotence. These fantasies become the core of his or her grandiose conception of the self, and lead to a blind optimism in his or her powers that make him or her ready to accept total independence from others. Other people are perceived as threatening and unreliable, and to survive, the child must become independent of those others. Splitting makes it impossible for the child to acknowledge his or her own aggression, or to show concern for others.

The memories that lie at the heart of the narcissistic personality, hovering on the borderline of neurosis and psychosis, are the memories of primitive aggression on the one hand and inadequate 'good objects' on the other. These memories lead to profound shame, lack of self-worth, fear of rage and horror of rejection.

The narcissistic personality has some characteristics which make it identifiable. Such people need to be loved and see others only in relation to themselves. They have a very inflated idea of their own importance and superiority (which alternates with feelings of overwhelming inferiority) and find empathic feelings for others difficult. Their relationships tend to be exploitative and they need a great deal of admiration from others, whom, conversely, they mistrust and deprecate. The narcissistic personality is an extreme form of chronic shame, but its origins are not too dissimilar to those of other forms of chronic shame.

Social Origins of Shame

The twentieth century was the century, among other things, of psychological explanations of human behaviour. Earlier generations would have seen shame arising, not from early childhood, but from the experiences which the psychotherapeutic model identifies as later triggers to a pre-existing disposition to feelings of shame.

In cultures where honour is significant, self identity is intimately connected with fulfilling the expectations of that society. To be dishonoured means not just feeling an acute sense of embarrassment, but becoming disconnected from the very social fabric in which the code of honour is embedded:

> Loss of honour . . . means dropping out of an entire system of exchange, of mutual perception or recognition: nobody knows how to talk to you any longer . . . in such cultures shame is both a personal and a social penalty: it is not just a particularly acute form of embarrassment, which I may brazen out or which I hope will be forgotten, but a real restriction on what I am able to think and feel about myself, as much as on what others think of me, make of me, say to me and understand about me.[7]

As I write this the world is convulsed in what has been dubbed 'the war on terrorism', or what looks suspiciously like a war upon Islam to many adherents to that faith. Most observers see the roots of this conflict in the plight of the Palestinians in the Middle East, and in a culture where dishonour and pride are significant social determinants. The prolonged subservience of Palestinian Arabs to the military grip of Israel led to the intifadas and the depth of anger and shame which generates suicide bombers. Osama Bin Laden objects to the presence of 'infidels' on holy territory, by which he means American troops stationed in Saudi Arabia, the land of his birth, and so shaming is this that a jihad, or holy war is the only honourable response. Neither can we ignore the sense of outrage and injured pride in the response of the United States to the September 11th terrorist attacks on Washington and New York in 2001.

On the domestic scale, in cultures where honour is more important than the values of compassion and forgiveness, retribution for slighted honour accounts for the killing and disfiguring of women in Pakistan and Bangladesh. It seems significant to me that this abuse of women is sometimes by means of acid thrown at their faces or over their bodies. Having 'lost face', men seek to destroy the faces of those whom they perceive as having dishonoured them.

Shame and guilt, then, are used as signals to control the boundaries of social behaviour. An old punishment for misdemeanours was the stocks, where public shaming counted for as much as the discomfort of physical blows or being hit by rotten vegetables.

Shakespeare's King Lear is a figure who feels increasingly dishonoured by his daughters as they assume control over the lands he has disposed of. In Act I Scene IV Albany asks Lear, 'What's the matter, Sir?' Addressing his daughter, Goneril, Lear replies:

> 'I'll tell thee: Life and death! I am ashamed
> That thou hast power to shake my manhood thus;
> That these hot tears, which break from me perforce,
> Should make thee worth them. Blasts and fogs upon
> thee!'[8]

and later finding Kent in the stocks, Lear rages:

> 'They durst not do't,
> They could not, would not do't; 'tis worse than murther,
> To do upon respect such violent outrage.'[9]

Lear displays the signs of a narcissistic personality disorder! The events, however, are the social context for his sense of shame and vulnerability.

Pines[10] sees our Western culture varying from earlier or other cultures in the way it internalises shame:

> Our Western models of emotions serve the function of protecting individuated selves from dangerous and asocial acts of impulse, lust and violence. Our shame and guilt are part of ourselves, each of us carrying our internal police force. We are individuated sufficiently to fulfil the demands of our complex society which requires personal mobility. Guilt has become secularised as a watchful consciousness, divorced from an absolute deity, now obliging persons to render account to society for themselves and their deeds.

The Western cultural model can be contrasted with those cultures and societies where the social controls on behaviour have not been replaced by the 'internalised police' of Western, post-Enlightenment liberalism. An extreme example might be the religious police of the former Taliban regime in Afghanistan or the Saudi *mutawwain*, whose seeming misogyny the West finds so hard to comprehend. Where shame is ignored, overridden or protracted without recompense, societies turn to violence and anger in what Scheff[11] calls a 'shame–rage spiral'.

There are other approaches to shame. Pattison[12] outlines philosophical, literary and social constructivist approaches in addition to those discussed above. He does not prioritise any one approach over another, remaining formally agnostic about the epistemologies of each, and treating all discourses, whatever their origins, as equal. This has the advantage of allowing the various voices to be heard in the discussion of the complex phenomenon of shame. However, my own personal journey nudges me towards a less agnostic approach, and my assumption is that shame as a human phenomenon finds its origins in basic biological mechanisms in the infant, but that cultural and social particularities amplify or dampen the experience of shame on the macro level, whilst the personal story of individuals has a similar effect on the micro, or personal, level. Thus, any attempts to alleviate the harmful and de-humanising effects of excessive shame will need to pay attention to both the cultural and the personal levels. I also believe that the message of the Christian faith has some significance at both levels in its potential to bring relief and wholeness, whilst its abuses must also be exposed at both levels.

Spiritual Approaches to Shame

A third set of causes of shame derives its power from our very creatureliness and finitude. We are a subtle blend of body and spirit, earth and heaven, dust and fire; made in the image of God for a relationship with him, but with that relationship shattered by sin. However, that hunger for eternity, a longing for the Other, remains, and can become twisted into shame.

There is also an awareness within many people of their smallness, not just in the normal run of events and history, but in terms of the vastness and unimaginable age of the universe. The Hebrew Bible echoes this sense of finitude:

> To whom will you liken God . . .
> It is he who sits above the circle of the earth,
> and its inhabitants are like grasshoppers;
> who stretches out the heavens like a curtain . . .
>
> (Isaiah 40:18, 22)

> As for mortals, their days are like grass;
> they flourish like a flower of the field;
> for the wind passes over it and it is gone,
> and its place knows it no more.
>
> (Psalm 103:15–16)

This sense of being overwhelmed, of awe at the vastness of things can become a vital aspect of the worship of God, as we sense his greatness and wonder. However, it can also become a twisted thing, resulting in self-loathing and shame. Perhaps a vital factor in determining which way the inbuilt sense of awe will turn, to wonder or to shame, lies in the upbringing and shaping of a human life at an early stage.

One of my early experiences of being overwhelmed and awestruck came during a visit to one of the great Gothic cathedrals as a young boy. My parents and I were on holiday, no doubt, and stepping through the door used every day by visitors and worshippers on the west front (a much more modest affair than the mighty west door itself) into the vast space inside, with its soaring piers and ribbed vault, I was almost scared to go further, giddy with wonder. Never before had I seen such a huge space (somehow, the outside world, familiar from birth, was not a threat). Of course, that was one of the aims of the builders three-quarters of a millennium ago; to instil a sense of awestruck wonder, or perhaps of control and fear, into the lives of ordinary English men and women. It certainly worked for me! I cannot now enter a cathedral with the same degree of awareness of my finitude, but a hint or echo of that early experience remains, now rationalised into wonder at the skill and ingenuity of the master masons who built such glorious buildings.

This sense of awe, the numinous, or 'cosmic dread', lies close to the psychological roots of religious experience, and is not the exclusive preoccupation of religious people, be they Christians or Jews, Muslims or Hindus. This experience is widespread, and is often voiced in terms of wonder at the natural realm, particularly since the Romantic movement gave special weight to the majestic and the rugged in nature. William Wordsworth writes of suddenly encountering an unexpected cliff while rowing a boat at night as a boy, an experience which haunts his waking moments and his dreams.

> . . . my Boat
> Went heaving through the water, like a Swan;
> When from behind that craggy Steep, till then
> The bound of the horizon, a huge Cliff,
> As if with voluntary power instinct,
> Uprear'd its head . . .
>
> . . . With trembling hands I turn'd,
> And through the silent water stole my way
>
> . . . And after I had seen
> That spectacle, for many days, my brain
> Work'd with a dim and undetermin'd sense
> Of unknown modes of being; in my thoughts
> There was a darkness, call it solitude,
> Or blank desertion . . .
>
> . . . But huge and mighty Forms that do live
> Like living men mov'd slowly through my mind
> By day and were the trouble of my dreams.[13]

People experience such powerful responses but rarely. More familiar is wonder at a fiery sunset, mountain grandeur or distant vista. Our very familiarity with images of the natural world, seen in books or television screen, or painted by artists such as J. M. W. Turner, has diminished the 'shock' factor that underlay the response of earlier generations, unprepared as they were for scenery that seemed to dwarf them. Nonetheless, the possibility of that sense of awe remains, and is a contributory aspect of the numinous. Allied to a sense of self-diminishment, such awe turns to shame when not directed to the purpose of worship. That 'worship' might remain fixed at the level of the natural world, or it might be transformed into the worship of a transcendent Deity. The Bible suggests that 'shameless' behaviour is ultimately derived from a failure to worship the Creator, substituting instead the worship of the creature (Rom. 1:18–27). In short, misdirected wonder and awe can produce shame, in that there is a longing to worship God shaped in the soul of humanity, a longing that turns to shame when not allowed its proper object.

CHAPTER 4

Shame and Postmodern Culture

WE SAW IN the previous chapter that there are psychological and spiritual roots for shame, roots which transcend particular cultures. We also looked at the social roots of shame in those cultures where honour and dishonour are powerful tools of social conditioning and understanding. Shame is an experience which is actively nurtured in those cultures, whereas in the West it has been viewed far more negatively, as something to be eradicated. Indeed, some might argue that there is too little shame in Western postmodern culture. People can act with impunity in ways which previous generations would call 'shameful'. This lack of 'discretion' shame, as we called it in the Introduction, is remarkable to members of, say, a Pakistani rural Muslim community.

To live for any length of time in Britain today, with access to the media, produces a familiarity with the naked human form unheard of only fifty years ago. Sexual images and allure are used to sell almost everything in advertising and, while we do not want to risk sounding like 'Disgusted of Tunbridge Wells', such over-use dulls the impact after a while. From perfume and clothes (when we might expect explicitly sexual imagery to be used), to mobile phone networks and a fast food snack (when we might not), images that lack discretion are ubiquitous.

The shame associated with betrayal of public trust is another area in which a proper use of social shame has been undermined. Politicians, government ministers and senior managers in public bodies such as health trusts and utilities

owe a duty of responsibility to the wider community. When
they betray trust, act dishonourably or lie, the shame of the
exposure of that betrayal used to result in a resignation.
Rowan Williams argues that remorse is one of the major
cultural bereavements of our age.[1] In place of remorse, the
shamed person might turn to therapy to help him or her feel
strong at the time of tension. The loss of discretion shame
leaves a vacuum filled by human willing:

> A culture which tolerates the loss of a sense of damage to
> the moral identity, the loss of shame or remorse, is bound
> to be one that dangerously overplays the role of the will
> in the construction of human persons.[2]

There is still a legacy of desire for a political culture in
which those who hold power relinquish it if they act
immorally, lie to the public (or to Parliament), or if their
department makes a gross error. Somehow, there is still an
expectation that the minister responsible will 'do the decent
thing' and resign, but the politicians who would meet those
expectations are few. Remorse and shame are secondary to
the will for power.

In this chapter about the origin of the narcissistic culture
of postmodernism I want to explore some commonplace
experiences of toxic shame: the way in which postmodern
spirituality disengaged from religious belief produces shame;
the legacy of childish and sentimental adulthood that is produced by not allowing children to be childish; and the culture
of narcissism that postmodernism creates.

Commonplace Social Shame

Postmodern culture, more than its immediate predecessor,
modernism, is a culture of disparate groups and 'tribes'. The
fragmentation of society associated with the loss of
confidence in the all-embracing myth of modern progress
and rationality upon which modernism was built has

resulted in groups of people that identify with a variety of more 'local' stories. This is nowhere more common than amongst teenagers, predictably so when at that developmental stage peer group approval is paramount. Punks, goths, indies, surfers, ravers . . . the list of subgroups grows apace. Each has its favoured music, dress codes, values and activities.[3] Each has its own culture, a culture which is 'ordinary' or 'popular'.[4] Stuart Hall views these subcultures as acts of resistance against the dominant culture, exploited for purposes of social control by the economically and socially dominant group.[5] Thus, skinhead identity, Hall argued, is characterised by working-class resistance to unemployment and immigration. Others have criticised the male perspective and demonstrated that young women use shopping to create identity. Certainly for both sexes, dress is a powerful means of expressing culture and group belonging, often with a desire to shock the status quo. Thus goths utilise the symbols of vampirism and death, with echoes of sado-masochism derived from punks (bondage gear) to create the group visual identity. To be evicted or excluded from the group, which expresses the desires and aspirations of the individual, leads to a sense of alienation, inferiority and dejection that is associated with shame. The threat of exclusion becomes a powerful motivation to conform to the group *mores*.

The alternative to group membership can sometimes be more destructive even than exclusion. Amongst schoolchildren and in the workplace, bullying can become endemic. The sense of fear and shame associated with being bullied can lead to depression and suicide. Bullying by those in positions of power is especially heinous: managers in the workplace or teachers in school who use ridicule and violence to enforce compliance are part of a shame-inducing culture. It is also employed by some whose job is to care for the most vulnerable adults, such as those who have dementia and are cared for in institutional settings. Here, Kitwood[6] includes 'treachery, disempowerment, infantilisation, intimidation, labelling, stigmatisation, invalidation of the person, banishment, objectification, ignoring, imposition, withholding, accusation, mockery and disparagement' as aspects of a malignant social psychology which exacerbates the condition of dementia and generates toxic shame.

On a broader scale, shame is felt by those groups within society that are marginalised and largely excluded from positions of control or power. Black and Asian people, women and the mentally ill are still noticeable for their exclusion from positions traditionally (and currently) held by white, middle-class, articulate men. The inclusion of a black minister in the cabinet in the Blair Government's second term (in 2002 Paul Boateng was appointed to the cabinet as a Treasury minister) was deemed remarkable because he was the first black African ever to hold that post. The appointment of bishops in the Church of England goes largely unnoticed unless they are black.

Such marginalisation is a form of institutionalised racism, and racism produces shame in its victims. The response is most often to hide, but the media make much more of those who respond by inverting the shaming, in the way Robert Mugabe, President of Zimbabwe, has acted against white farmers; or by finding the strength in solidarity to be proud of the very attributes which the dominant culture derides: their race, gender or sexuality. Thus, for instance, the rise of the Black Power movement and the Nation of Islam in the United States, the feminist movement and Gay Pride groups.

Shamed people are withdrawn, want to hide, and do not often 'rock the boat' or pose a threat. They are useful to have around if a society wants to ensure conformity. As we shall see later, religious groups and churches are not immune to the social abuse of shaming mechanisms, and can be amongst the most irresponsible manipulators of others by the use of shame.

Spirituality and Religion

In postmodern society spirituality is acceptable, desirable even. However, religious affiliation or belief is as bemusing and worthy of derision to the majority as ever it was in modernism.

If one of the means of maintaining healthy levels of discretion shame, together with an absence of toxic shame, is through close and vulnerable human relationships ('fellowship', to use the Christian jargon), whereby the individual is recognised, valued, comforted and respected by the group in which he/she is included, then the current subversion of religious faith and belonging into spirituality that is primarily individualistic can only exacerbate levels of shame.

The Harvard sociologist Robert Putnam noted how in America more people than ever are going ten-pin bowling, but fewer are joining clubs and leagues, and coined the phrase 'bowling alone' to describe the phenomenon throughout the Western world in which fewer people are joining clubs or societies. Jonathan Sacks reflects on this phrase:

> It is the triumph of the self over the group, the 'Me' over the 'Us', the lonely individual without commitments and attachments replacing the faithful spouse, the responsible parent, the loyal colleague, the member of a community. Spirituality is what happens when religion goes 'Bowling Alone'.[7]

If in the Western soul spirituality is good and religion is bad, then it might be argued that at least it shows we are not just materialist consumers undergoing retail therapy. But actually it just consumerises and privatises genuine faith. To discover spiritual realities is not difficult, but to translate them into the public world is hard, and that is what the great religions do. They translate private spiritual experience into public action for justice and peace:

39

To discover God within the soul is easy. What is hard is to bring God into the world, with all its poverty, inequality, violence and terror, and make it a home for His presence by celebrating His image in others.

That takes real work, the long, hard, steady work of love in action, loyalty in deed, generosity to those who are different from you, and commitment to those who do not yet share your blessings.[8]

Because spirituality avoids these hard choices, which include rejecting actions which lead to toxic shame in others and developing social policies that are inclusive and committed to face-to-face human relationships, its rise is not necessarily a sign of a less shaming culture. Indeed, quite the reverse, for individualism lacks the social fellowship which helps to remove shame and the religious context to transform anew into healthy worship and avoid the turn to cosmic shame.

Children in Postmodern Culture

The term 'toxic shame' was first coined to describe the kind of impact upon children of a family system organised to cope with an adult member who is in the grip of drug or alcohol dependency, or who systematically abuses their spouse or children physically, emotionally or sexually. Such toxic shame, with its poisonous miasma of fear, guilt and shame, is responsible for the more obvious damage to children in abusing or dysfunctional homes. However, there is also the wider culture of narcissism which has its more diffuse impact upon most of our children, growing up in a society where those values and aspirations are the cultural norm.

Throughout the second half of August 2002 the attention of Britain was gripped by the unfolding tragedy played out on television screens from a quiet country town in Cambridgeshire: Soham. The abduction and murder of two ten-year-old schoolgirls, Jessica Chapman and Holly Wells, shocked a society almost inured to the casual violence experienced by children week in and week out in homes across the country, the maiming and beating of children on the streets of Belfast as paramilitary gangs mete out rough justice as they attempt to keep a hold over the communities they abuse and exploit, and the abduction of children (over 600 children were abducted in Britain in 2001).

The Soham case and those like it: Sarah Payne's murder in Sussex; Damilola Taylor's death on the Peckham Park Estate; the horrific abuse and murder of Victoria Climbié, highlighted what is still mercifully rare and focused attention upon what is one of the greatest of tragedies, the needless death of a child. The response of the public to this tragedy: gifts of flowers and teddy bears and messages expressing grief and bewilderment (many asked the question, 'why?') reminded me of the death of Princess Diana. It touched something deep and widespread in our society. The media helped, of course, to give those deaths iconic status, but our reaction as a nation revealed a deep ambivalence in our attitude to children.

This unease is nothing new, as a story from the Gospel of Luke (18:15–17) reveals. Luke, following Mark's original account in Mark 10, tells a simple story. Recognising who Jesus is, parents are bringing their little children to him in an echo of the custom of bringing children to be blessed by the scribes and teachers of the law on the eve of the Day of Atonement, Yom Kippur. Children are of little value in first-century Palestine. Adults are important, but children are just adults-in-waiting, and the disciples are indignant that the time and energy of the Master, Jesus, should be absorbed in so insignificant an interruption. He has far more important things to do than waste his time with children!

However, Jesus rebukes his own disciples, for no one is unimportant to God, and so no one is unimportant to Jesus. Like women, sinners, tax-collectors, publicans and whores, those who are least significant in the eyes of the important assume greatest significance in the eyes of Jesus. He would far sooner welcome and bless a child than keep company with a self-righteous bigot like the Pharisee in the preceding parable (18:9–14).

No, says Jesus, children are important, precisely because they are children and not adults, and it is their very childishness, their trusting nature, vulnerability and dependence that are the attitudes needed if strong, cynical and suspicious adults are to enter the Kingdom of God. Nothing is more touching than a little child asleep on its mother's shoulder, and few things more ridiculous than a grown adult attempting the same posture, thumb in mouth! Yet, it is that trust which Jesus highlights.

If the society of Jesus' day was guilty of treating children as not-yet-human, as being of less worth than they have in God's eyes, our own culture has adopted a different twisting of their true worth and status. While children are certainly of equal worth to adults in God's eyes, whether or not they are yet born, they are not of *greater* worth. The unnecessary aborting of children is one of the great evils of our day, treating a foetus as if it is not yet human, but those whose passion for the unborn leads them to murder the doctors and nursing staff who undertake abortions rob that cause of much of its moral credibility. One of the curious twists of our post-modern society is that we idolise children, and correspondingly demonise abusers of children.

A second curious twist is that we rob children of their freedom to be irresponsible: we ask them to make choices about what they will consume as they are bombarded with advertising about this or that toy, food (usually highly processed and over-full of sugar and salt, which is harmful to their health) or item of clothing. As Rowan Williams has written:

> Anything but innocuous is the conscription of children into the fetishistic hysteria of style wars: it is still merci-

fully rare to murder for a pair of trainers, or to commit suicide because of an inability to keep up with peer group fashion; but what can we say about a marketing culture that so openly feeds and colludes with obsession?[9]

We make children economic consumers because the postmodern gods are the market and the bottom line. Children need to be free from such concerns if they are to grow into mature adults, and part of the price we pay for our twistedness is a generation of adults who are childish, disabled in their choice-making and poorly equipped to nurture children because they are not secure in their adult freedoms. Such childish adults are prone to shame-inducing childrearing.

Thirdly, we habitually sexualise children, and not just through the alarming rates of sexual abuse prevalent in our culture. The language of desire is learned even before the nature of that desire is quite understood. At its most crass is the existence of children's beauty contests in the USA, where the stereotypes of predatory male and seductive female are happily exploited and thought touching in children of six to eight years old. A young adult woman, perhaps understandably, dresses to impress the opposite sex. But when we mimic her alluring clothes in the style of clothes for a child of seven, we abuse the freedom of children to be children. We impose upon them a burden of meaning and significance that children ought not to bear.

Note the contrast with Jesus, who accepts children for who they are not for their economic potential or their desirability, nor even for the potential adults that they will become. Simply, they are the objects of God's love and care.

When we routinely and unthinkingly do these twisted things to children almost everywhere in our society, perhaps we should not be so surprised when sick and evil adults fail to honour the bond of trust that we have in the care of children and use and abuse them. They are only taking to an extreme conclusion with one or two unfortunate children what our society does routinely to them all, treating them like little adults in the service of our needs and those of our gods, the free market and the profit motive. Children growing up in such a culture will be especially prone to insecurity, bullying and sexual dysfunction, all ripe for producing shame-filled adults.

Shame and Cultural Narcissism

James Fowler has written:

> . . . though shame has been more invisible in Western societies in this century, especially in the United States, it pervades our personal and collective lives in ways that underlie a great deal of the self-destructive and violent patterns of our society. Moreover, shame plays a central role in the high rates of depression and of substance abuse among us.[10]

One dimension of postmodern society is the challenge of including the excluded, those who lack the economic muscle to participate in the material benefits of a consumer culture. An underclass is apparent in North-Atlantic societies where, devoid of the support of family, community, church or school, young people are pushed beyond the limits of social shame into a 'shameless' life of violence, drug addiction and prostitution. The shame felt by those who do not have what a consumer-led culture says everyone can have, and needs to have, to find worth and value is too great to bear.

Even those aspects of contemporary British social and political life that are intended to improve the quality of service provision, precisely with the disadvantaged in mind, can inadvertently cultivate a culture of shame. Inner city schools where literacy rates are low due to a preponderance of pupils for whom English is their second or third language find themselves near the bottom of school league tables, and labelled as 'failing schools'. There was at one stage talk of 'naming and shaming' such failing schools. Late in 2002, the quality of service provision by local authorities was assessed across a range of criteria. Those with a grade 1 assessment were deemed to be successful, and relieved of the imposition of such assessment exercises for a five-year period, while those with a grade 4 assessment were to be more closely monitored. For such councils, an already demoralised work-force had to bear the shame of working in a failing council. Such councils are hardly likely to attract the best candidates for posts, and so the cycle of failure is perpetuated. With over thirty separate assessment criteria to be reported upon and examined, senior managers spend less time improving the quality of the service and more time working on the assessment programme, further limiting the possibility of improving the delivery of services to their communities. It seems as if this culture of assessment, with its endemic propensity to shame, takes as its text the words of Jesus, 'For to all those who have, more will be given, and they will have an abundance; but from those who have nothing, even what they have will be taken away' (Matt. 25:29). I am sure Jesus was not thinking of a market-driven culture when he told the parable of the talents, but he certainly summed up one of its more damaging characteristics.

James Fowler describes four distortions of healthy shame, and applies them primarily to individuals.[11] There is a case, however, for applying these distortions to the wider cultural experience of shame that reinforces a culture of narcissism. His four distortions are:

1. perfectionist shame
2. shame due to enforced minority status
3. toxic shame
4. shamelessness.

Perfectionist shame

Perfectionist shame has its origins in the childhood of the individual who needs to gain the approval of those it is most dependent upon by meeting their values and conforming to their behaviours. It is vital that the child wins this approval in order to enforce its own security, for care and love is perceived by that child to be conditional upon conformity. A client of mine described how four of her childhood friends 'ran away' from home (not together, but on separate occasions) and in at least one case the police were called to look for the absconding child. While she perceives her home to be far more abusive than those of her friends, and the provocation to run away more intense, she remained the conforming 'good' child. 'I was far too scared to run away' she said, 'I would not have dared.' Instead she endured the abuse and conformed in an attempt to win the approval of the care-givers and avoid the inevitable retribution had she run away.

Fowler says that perfectionist shame has its roots in the first year of life, and inconsistent or inadequate mirroring by the primary care-giver (which might be due to depression, distraction, or the emotional or physical absence of that care-giver). John could not tolerate imperfection in his own life, and his reputation as an engineer of exacting standards, working at very fine tolerances, spilled over into his attitude to his children. Anything less than an A grade was a failure, and woe betide them if they were not at the top of the class. As those family relationships began to break down under the intolerable pressure of his domineering perfectionism, he sought some help. His family history revealed that his mother had suffered a period of postnatal depression from four to eight months after John's birth, and a succession of different care-givers who supported John's mother were unable to replicate or substitute the consistent mirroring that she otherwise might have been able to provide. The clumsy mirroring from a variety of faces resulted in the creation of a false self within John as, in his second year of life, his experience of being evaluated by those who mattered (primarily his now recovered mother) was biased in the direction of an anxious and self-critical sensitivity towards their approval. This false identity was reinforced by his mother's own anxiety that her period of depression had resulted in a developmental delay in John, and she compensated by pushing his development of language, and especially his control of his bladder (potty training), in ways that resulted in John seeking to fulfil, indeed exceed those expectations. John also succeeded in other socialising environments such as play group, school and scouts, always eager to please and impress: a 'model' pupil. It was only in his adult life, with the crisis of a rebellious and non-conforming family around him, that he began to explore the reasons for his obsessive need for achievement in himself and, by extension, those he had created, his own children.

If this is the individual's experience, what kind of generalised shame is created in our culture of perfectionism, with its pressures of work as we compete in a global market? In such a market only the best survive, so perfectionism becomes endemic. Education is reduced to gaining good grades in order to gain a place at one of the better universities, in order to achieve the level of professional excellence which guarantees a good income and secure future. Indeed, such a culture of achievement leads to the obscenity of four-year-olds in kindergarten being drilled in literacy and numeracy in order to gain a competitive edge over their fellows, rather than being allowed to do what four-year-olds do best, learn through play.

Shame due to enforced minority status

Between eighteen months and two years of age, self-awareness develops. The child becomes aware that the image in the mirror is actually him or herself. As that self-awareness develops it is extremely sensitive to the valuation of others, and the way in which parents pass on their own sense of social shame if they are in a disadvantaged minority (a racial or religious minority group for instance) is powerful in the shaping of the child's own self-estimation. This ascribed shame results from the social environment's devaluing of certain qualities (such as skin colour or dress code) over which both the child and its family have little or no control. Of particular power is the devaluing of the female gender in a patriarchal society, so that girls commonly grow up with a loss of self-esteem due to their gender alone. Boys are important, girls are rubbish, is the message imbibed from these early years.

Fowler notes that this kind of shame cannot be healed without attending to the social and economic forces that create discrimination. The social applications of this kind of shame are obvious. It is the shame of finding oneself the only black child in a white school, at the mercy of the cruelties of playground taunts unmodified by the positive side of political correctness, which in adult contexts would never dream of drawing attention to a person's skin colour. It is the shame of discovering that you are attracted to people of the same sex in a school where the ultimate accusation is to be called 'gay'. It is the shame of wearing Marks & Spencer's trainers when everyone else wears Nike and New Balance. It takes enormous strength of character and huge resources of parental approval and pride to counter the insidious effects of being different and disadvantaged.

Toxic shame

The child growing up in a family where the father is an alcoholic soon learns that survival depends upon their conforming to a family system that is designed to simultaneously support and belittle the father. At home they must support the mother in her continual devaluing and criticism of their father's behaviour, but at the same time, beyond the home, they must be a staunch advocate for him, denying the shameful behaviour and addiction which is alcoholism. 'In these kinds of situations the "false self" is on stage most of the time in a person's life. The core of the self is built around shaping and maintaining a public posture that contradicts in many ways the everyday realities of the child's life.'[12] The resulting splits and distortions create a 'broken heart', where added to the lack of mirroring in the early years and the abuse experienced in later childhood is a pattern of family life which suppresses truth and denies reality.

Applying this to a wider cultural context, toxic shame might lie behind the growth in mental health problems that our society faces.

Narcissistic Culture

Christopher Lasch catches the prevailing *zeitgeist* well in his seminal work, *The Culture of Narcissism*.[13] 'The contemporary climate is therapeutic, not religious. People today hunger not for personal salvation, let alone for the restoration of an earlier golden age, but for the feeling, the momentary illusion, of personal well-being.' He argues that a culture of narcissistic self-absorption dominated the late twentieth century. This is echoed in a change in the kinds of patholo-gical disorders encountered by therapists and psychiatrists in their consulting rooms. What hysteria and obsessive–compulsive disorders were to Freud at the beginning of the twentieth century, the narcissistic disorders are to the work-aday analyst in the latter decades of that century. 'Today's patients by and large do not suffer from hysterical paralyses of the legs or hand-washing compulsions; instead it is their very psychic selves that have gone numb or that they must scrub and rescrub in an exhausting and unending effort to come clean.'[14]

The narcissist that Lasch identifies as the cultural norm in late twentieth-century America is aware of his own condition, anxious about health, fearful of ageing and death, unable to mourn and sexually promiscuous. America's success was built upon the Protestant work ethic, with its duty to contribute to the social good. The self-made man was the archetypal embodiment of the American dream, wedded to hard work, sobriety, moderation, freedom from debt and self-discipline. In an age of diminishing expectations, however, only fools put off till tomorrow the fun they can have today. The happy survivor replaces the industrious entrepreneur: Robinson Crusoe is replaced by Moll Flanders. The Puritans, with their God-fearing self-denial and service of others, who were the founding fathers of the colony, have been replaced by the republican vision of that most disturbing of the prophets of radical individualism, the Marquis de Sade. He defended unlimited self-indulgence as the logical outcome of the revolutionary capitalism of the new world of the Enlightenment. Pleasure becomes life's only business, no matter how depraved or violent.

The icon of the age of narcissism is the pop idol with his or her ambiguity towards fame. In Britain, the alternative royal family are Posh and Becks, Victoria and David Beckham, pop star and footballer, fashionable and famous. Every twist and turn of their lives is lived in the gaze of the media: even the location of the conception of their children is public knowledge (naming their first born Brooklyn rather gave the game away. It was fortunate that their second was not conceived in the Hertfordshire village not far from where I live, called Ugley). The long queues of young hopefuls who aspire to be picked as new pop idols or models; the banality of reality TV and the cult of celebrity represent the diminished expectations of a narcissistic culture. In part, such a cultural transformation will have an impact upon levels of shame and shamelessness, either increasing it or diminishing it. I believe that our current cultural turns can only increase levels of 'chronic' shame, both amongst those who fail to achieve their aspirations to be famous, and amongst those who pay the price of fame in the currency of such psychological disorders and mental health problems as anorexia, substance abuse and depression.

CHAPTER 5

Shame and Sex

O F ALL THE subjects about which Christians get 'hot under the collar', sex is probably the hottest. Over the past ten years British denominations have wrestled long and hard over the ethics of homosexuality; the large majority of those approaching a church minister with a request to conduct a wedding will already be sexual partners, if not actually cohabiting partners (and not a few will be parents), and the use of contraceptives is widespread, even amongst Catholics whose church forbids their use. These issues and practices are different from those of fifty years ago, and different again from those of five hundred or two thousand years ago. Yet, the experience of shame about sex is still a reality in our society, even after the two 'sexual revolutions' of the past fifty years: the revolution in permissiveness in the 1960s and 1970s ('sexual intercourse began in 1963'!); the new Puritanism brought on by the threat of AIDS in the 1980s, which was already waning in the late 1990s, and the widespread social acceptance of gays and lesbians in the metropolitan cultures of London, Manchester and elsewhere. The result of those trends has been a commodifying of sex and a loss of the expectation that intimacy within a relationship is a necessary precursor to sexual intimacy. This is not to suggest that most sexual activity does not take place within loving and stable relationships (it most likely does), but rather that such a relationship is optional to the idea of good sex, or perhaps, more generously, that such a relationship is preferable but not indispensable.

It is not surprising that the West has so often linked sex and shame, given the pervasive influence of Christianity, which itself has, at best, been ambivalent about sex, and at worst positively hostile. We have seen elsewhere the roots of this in a misinterpretation of the Genesis story of the Garden of Eden, with its linking of nakedness, shame and the eating of the fruit of the Tree of the Knowledge of Good and Evil. Augustine believed that the sexual act never occurs without concupiscence, and is implicitly sinful, while the avoidance of sex by those called to a celibate priesthood, and the apparently almost equal sinfulness of the enjoyment of sexual intimacy even by those legitimised to engage in it within the bounds of marriage, all bear witness to a strand within Western Christianity which thinks sex is messy and best avoided if possible. Rowan Williams points the finger at a homogenising of sexual norms by the early church through its proud claim that at least a substantial proportion of the early Christians renounced all sexual activity, be it marriage, sex with slaves, youthful sexual experimentation or the use of prostitutes. They did not think sex was evil so much as 'just a bit . . . undignified'.[1] Where sex is so strongly associated with guilt, shame is almost bound to be a close companion.

Angela Tilby reminds us of a scene in the film about fragmented sexual and romantic relationships, *When Harry Met Sally*.[2] The heroine, Sally, is complaining to her (at this stage platonic) friend Harry about her ex-boyfriend, who had noted that her designer knickers had the days of the week emblazoned on them, from Monday to Saturday. 'Where's Sunday?' he asks. Sally explains that they do not make Sunday knickers. Why not? Her answer, 'Because of God', says it all. God does not much like human beings having sex, it implies. Although sex is just about tolerable on weekdays, Sunday, being God's day, is a sex-free zone.

This seems a far cry from the rich use of sexual imagery in the Hebrew Scriptures (notably, of course, the Song of Solomon, a book which, while nowhere mentioning the name of God, has been deemed canonical and is often used by mystics as a deeply spiritual poem about the relationship of the believer to God), and an alternative Christian tradition, epitomised by the Eastern church. In Gregory of Nyssa we do not find the tortured conscience of an Augustine, but a much freer use of sexual imagery as a metaphor for communion with God. He affirms sexual intimacy, not as a sign of our fallen state, but rather as an anticipation of our eternal intimacy with God.

Changing Experience of Sexuality

If the experience of shame is a result in part of the social prohibitions and affirmations of what the majority see as 'normal' or acceptable, then we need to be aware of how fluid changing patterns of human sexuality and society's understanding of what is acceptable have been. The direction of trends is not always towards greater permissiveness, but the influence of postmodernism's contentment with the surface of things, rather than underlying truths or meanings, results in sex becoming a matter of good technique, fed by a diet of pseudo-educational articles in magazines (both men's and women's) and late-night programmes on the television, rather than a matter of loving relationship. Supposedly poor technique can quickly feed a sense of shame and inadequacy, as can the possession of a less-than-perfect body. The relentless pursuit of a flat stomach and perky breasts (or a six-pack torso and great biceps if you are a man), stimulated by the advertising industry and the publishers of glossy magazines, leaves many people feeling inadequate and ashamed of bodies with wrinkles and flab. They are the bodies that have been lived in. As Janet Morley puts it in her poem, they are the bodies of grownups.

> The bodies of grownups
> come with stretchmarks and scars
> faces that have been lived in,

relaxed breasts and bellies,
backs that give trouble
and well-worn feet . . .
And yet I think there is a flood of beauty
beyond the smoothness of youth[3]

Couple shame about a lived-in body with shame about sex
per se, and there is a powerful arena for chronic shame to
remain stubbornly fixed.

Discretion Shame and Sex

It is in the context of sex that the protective aspects of shame
are most obviously encountered. Freud saw one of the main
functions of shame as inhibiting basic drives associated with
forbidden aspects of sexuality. Of these, the visual taboos of
voyeurism and its corresponding alternative, exhibitionism,
were paramount. The one desired to see what should be kept
hidden (and underlies much of the world-wide business of
pornography), while exhibitionism desires to be seen. Shame
prevents most people acting upon immediate sexual desire,
and is an important control upon behaviour that is generally
accepted to be damaging to the good ordering of society, and
not least the safety of women. It is when this restraint is
removed, where shame is disallowed its proper function, that
chaos and harm ensue, and this is particularly so in the midst
of armed conflict, especially those brutal ethnic wars in
Africa or the Balkans when the enemy's women are
dehumanised. In the Rwandan massacres of 1992, many
women were raped and deliberately infected with HIV, as all
sense of restraint shame was removed in the madness of that
crisis. A decade on, the children born to those women are
themselves now dying of AIDS.

The Theological Problem

Part of the problem is a theological one. The Western church has generally favoured an understanding of the relationship between creation and redemption which is epitomised by Augustine. Put at its simplest (and this does not do justice to the subtlety of Augustine's theology) God creates a perfect universe and perfect humanity inhabits it, but with the rebellion against God that is told in the story of the Fall comes imperfection which embraces all of creation. God through his Son redeems the whole of creation which is restored to its original perfection, a return to Paradise. Within this scheme, sexual distinction, male and female, is part of the original perfection, and will remain in the restoration of all things that is the goal of redemption. The sexual organs remain, but shall no longer be put to 'carnal' use in intercourse and child-bearing, or excite that old enemy of purity of life, lust, but rather praise to God.[4] The problem with this conception is that sexual distinction remains part of what it is to be human. Indeed, some would say that it is at the core of our humanity. We are essentially and necessarily sexual beings. In some forms of this model of the relationship between creation and redemption, the Fall is essentially about a sexual awakening, and an awareness that sex is shamefully linked with the discovery of good and evil.

The alternate tradition comes from Irenaeus of Lyons, through Gregory of Nyssa and Gregory of Nazianzus (two of the Cappadocian Fathers), and this older tradition gives a rather different account of the relationship between creation and redemption. Using the concept of recapitulation, Irenaeus does not simply talk about a restoration to the original perfection of creation. Rather, what is perfected is different to what was lost. It is not simply that Christ assumes the fallen humanity of Adam to restore it to Adam's originality, but that Adam is created with the goal of being perfected in the image of the eternal Son. The incarnation is not then plan B once plan A has failed, but was plan A all along; the image of Christ is the goal of creation, and humanity is defined by the *imago Dei* which is Christ, rather than some particular aspect of humanity which distinguishes it from the rest of the animal realm, such as rationality. With this understanding, sexual distinction is not ultimate, but provisional. Human identity is ultimately not defined by gender distinction but rather in the ascended humanity of Christ. This *imago Dei* in Christ must therefore not be seen as a masculine image, further confirming the patriarchal bias in theology against which feminist theologians have rightly railed: rather, since God is beyond gender, redeemed humanity will be beyond gender.

This enables us to think of sexuality from a theological point of view as neither inherently shameful, nor as the individualistic characteristic it has become since the Enlightenment, but rather as an aspect of created humanity that is transcended in Christ. This is contrasted with the cultural weight placed upon the sexual act, whereby orgasm is almost the only remaining moment of transfiguration and transcendence left to a culture devoid of spirituality.

What follows from this is a theology of sexual intimacy which mirrors provisionally the fuller intimacy of sharing in the divine life (the sharing in the intimacy of Father, Son and Spirit which we share in Christ through the Spirit). Thus, the faithfulness, care and love of a man and wife in marriage anticipates the care and love of Christ, and the expression of that in sexual intimacy is but one means of expression. All genuine human loving which is not primarily self-gratifying or self-seeking, but rather self-giving, points to that ultimate intimacy of communion in Christ. This might seem to open up the way for same-sex relationships to be in some way anticipatory of the divine love, and indeed those who advocate the validity of same-sex relationships would strongly advocate this. I would also want to affirm the appropriateness of intimate friendship and partnership between same-sex couples as much as between hetero-sexuals, but would want to avoid the conclusion that genital sexual activity is necessarily obligatory. If our sexuality is provisional and not ultimate, then the expression of it is a secondary issue. Indeed it is only, perhaps, in response to the wider culture's obsession with sexual performance and prac-tice (a replacement of the disciplines of prayer as a means of transcendence by the disciplines of multi-orgasmic sex) that the church has become as obsessed as it is with the sleeping arrangements of same-sex couples. After all, in the 1970s, without a trace of irony, before the widespread impact of the militant gay movement, the most popular comedy act, Morecambe and Wise (two men) could regularly include the device of them in bed together, wearing pyjamas and dis-cussing life as if they were an old couple. There was no hint that they were lovers, and neither was it felt necessary to somehow explicitly state they were not.

Sex makes us vulnerable, and vulnerability is a terrifying challenge to the degree of control needed by the chronically ashamed, for it unmasks them. We become helpless, or out of control, driven by desire. We also discover that our bodies can be a source of happiness to ourselves and to another, and that is problematic for the ashamed, because they see them-selves as repulsive to others, or to themselves. Remember how Narcissus rejects the desire of Echo, and falls in love, not with the tangible body of another, but with the intangible reflection of himself, ever dissolving into ripples as he bends to kiss those lips that smile back at him. The Christian life 'has its rationale – if not invariably its practical reality – the task of teaching us so to order our relations that human beings may see themselves as desired, as the occasion of joy' writes Rowan Williams,[5] and it is the vulnerability of being available to the other as a source of their joy which consti-tutes the true reciprocity of lovemaking:

For my body to be the cause of joy, the end of home-coming, for me, it must be there for someone else, must be perceived, accepted, nurtured. And that means being given over to the creation of joy in that other, because only as directed to the enjoyment, the happiness, of the other does it become unreservedly loveable. To desire my joy is to desire the joy of the one I desire: my search for enjoyment through the bodily presence of another is a longing to be enjoyed in my body.[6]

This being given over to the joy of another carries with it risks of rejection and repulsion: we then read off our bodies the experience of shame. Two kinds of observers of sexuality avoid this risk: the pornographer, whose interest is in power and domination, and the technician, whose goal is maximising the muscular tensions and release of orgasm. Neither are able to understand the body's grace and its potential to dissolve shame in unreserved acceptance.

If an experience of desire and being desired is problematic for the shamed, then I believe that the discovery that I am desirable to the one whom I desire has in itself a healing dimension from the tendency to toxic shame in those who have known mostly rejection rather than acceptance in their relations hitherto.

CHAPTER 6

Shame and Depression

THOSE FOR WHOM shame has become toxic sometimes present to the helping professions, such as a GP, counsellor or pastor, with symptoms of depression, and there may well be a diagnosis of a depressive illness in which shame plays a significant or even controlling role. Andrews has analysed the relationship between shame, sexual abuse and depression, a relationship described in narrative form in our story of Jane.[1] The intimate relationship between shame and depression, and the widespread incidence of depression (it is the most commonly experienced form of mental ill-health) warrants a closer look at this relationship.

Often issues of guilt are thought to be significant in cases of depression, but my experience echoes that of Mollon:

> my own impression is that if one enquires sympathetically into the preoccupations of depressed patients, one may find repetitive ruminations over shameful and narcissistically injurious events. The characteristics of the 'depressed personality' . . . narcissistic vulnerability, sensitivity to slights, insults, criticisms and disappointments – may be seen in terms of proneness to shame.[2]

The therapy of choice in depression is rational–emotive therapy, a form of cognitive–interpersonal counselling. This assumes that depression has biochemical, social and psychological roots. All who suffer from depression have important biological factors associated with hormonal and biochemical changes, while the social context of the sufferer is important (poor housing, lack of social support and poorly managed trauma can be factors, for instance), as are experiences in early childhood which in later life disable a person from managing successfully developmental changes such as adolescence, menopause and contingent changes such as divorce or bereavement. The support and pastoral care of the depressed should recognise all three sets of factors.

While there are other approaches, from a reductionist approach which relies solely upon pharmacology (anti-depressants), to psychotherapeutic approaches which concentrate upon infancy, the evidence is that cognitive therapy is the most effective.[3] Its aim is to help the client to develop ways of thinking which are healthy and positive, replacing those thoughts which have become self-destructive. There are three basic concepts in cognitive counselling.[4]

1. **Automatic thoughts.** These are the immediate ideas and interpretations which spring to mind.
2. **Rules for living and basic attitudes.** These are the ideas and beliefs that guide our lives and set us in particular styles of living.
3. **Self–other schemata.** These represent internal organising systems that form the basis of our self-judgements and experiences on the one hand, and our judgements and experiences of other people on the other.

Cognitive models of helping focus upon the conscious relationship between thoughts and feelings. So, for instance, the client might be encouraged to 'catch' or monitor those automatic thoughts, to ruminate upon them and to evaluate whether they are appropriate. For example, if the client's partner arrives home from work tired and irritable and picks a fight over a trivial matter and the client's automatic thought is 'I am a bad and worthless person', the client will be helped to develop a more appropriate response: 'He has had a bad day.' Or if the automatic response to a failed examination is 'I will always fail at everything' (over-generalisation), then the client might be helped to respond with, 'I can pass this next time.' Other kinds of thought patterns which are associated with depression include magnification and minimisation (making errors in evaluating the importance and implication of events); personalisation (relating external events to the self with no rational basis) and absolutist, dichotomous thinking (something is all good or all bad). Working with these cognitive distortions is the basis of the initial therapeutic process, with the purpose of developing patterns of thinking which are less negative. The tone of thought is important. Often negative thoughts are articulated with anger, and it is important that the client does not replace one negative thought with another ('stop being so stupid to think this way'), but instead develops a more self-caring and supportive response with the help of the therapist.

The basic rules or beliefs are those ideas which govern the approach to life. In depressed people these are often distorted and dysfunctional. For instance, 'I must be perfect', 'I am worthless if that person does not like me', 'to be good and worthwhile, I must always put others' needs before my own'. These beliefs are learned in the home and culture, and some are distortions of religious beliefs. Thus, the Christian virtue of selflessness can be distorted into 'I am a bad person if I ever look after my own needs', or transposed in the narcissistic personality into 'only my needs are of any importance'. Here the therapist seeks to help the client evaluate those beliefs and rules, reinforcing the helpful and transforming the destructive.

Self–other schemata are the basic organising systems for knowledge about the self and others, built up through life as a result of interpersonal experience. A positive schema views the self and others as good, attractive, wanted, worthy, caring and competent, while a negative schema views self and others as unable, unattractive, worthless, etc. In cases of relatively uncomplicated depression, positive schemata are held in the memory although they are temporarily unavailable to the client. The switch to a negative schema is a temporary affair, with an expectation that with the end of the depression a switch to the positive schema will ensue. However, where depression is linked to shame and abuse or personality disorders, the positive schema is not present, or if present is extremely fragile. With no premorbid positive schema to tap into, the development of positive views of self and others must start from scratch, and the client–therapist relationship is particularly important in this role. Trust, reliability, warmth, honesty and empathy from the therapist become indispensable traits if a new identity is to be established in the client.

Putting this together, the case study of John illustrates how these three basic concepts interact.

John grew up as the youngest of three children. His older brothers were athletic, as was his father. Their achievements on the rugby pitch and cricket field were in stark contrast to his own indifference to sport. This, coupled with chronic asthma, left him feeling a failure in the eyes of the three family members whose approval he craved most. He grew up feeling he was a disappointment to his father and looked down upon by his elder brothers. He grew to be ashamed of his slight build and disappointed in his lack of sporting prowess, and became isolated from the games they played, avoiding the opportunity to be humiliated, as he perceived, by his clumsiness and weakness.

His **view of self** was *not good enough, not fit enough, a disappointment and a failure.*

His **view of others** was *rejecting, powerful, fit, able and demanding.*

By way of compensation, he developed his natural intellectual gifts, and used those achievements to ridicule his immediately older brother, who was intellectually lightweight. These patterns developed in adolescence, as John cultured a disdain for the athletes at school, sought the company and friendship of two other bright boys and used his wit and humour to defend himself. He affected a scruffy, bohemian manner, but his scurrilous wit alienated him from the mainstream of his school peers and his older brothers. He craved the approval of his friends as a way of deflecting the hunger for the approval from his father and brothers.

Basic attitudes and rules for living: *I must achieve intellectually to have any worth. Without academic success I will be rejected, not respected and ignored.*

My body is worthless and attention to personal hygiene or fashion is a sign of weakness.

At 17 he became infatuated with a girl in his class. She was bright and attractive, an intellectual achiever like himself, but unlike him, smart and well-liked by many. She liked his humour, but was not otherwise attracted to him sexually. Her rejection of his advances prompted a mental breakdown more profound than simply that of a disappointment in love.

Negative automatic thoughts: *In the only area that really matters (my physical body and sexual attractiveness) I am a failure. No one will love me. I am a freak. There is no point in trying to make myself attractive. Others despise me.*

His shame at his appearance and performance prompted a depressive illness characterised by a desire to hide and retreat from all company.

Cognitive–behavioural therapists sometimes use shame-attacking exercises with mild embarrassment, such as speaking to a stranger as if they were a friend, or wearing what, for the sufferer, would be outrageous dress, but in cases of severe depressive shame such shame-attacking exercises are counter-productive, only serving to intensify the shame and the desire to hide. Therapists need to take great care to avoid the production of a shame-inference chain.[5] The client does not want the counsellor to find out about some episode or story. 'If he/she finds out about that they will discover how bad a person I am, and then he/she will reject me. If they reject me, this will confirm how bad I really am. But if I do not disclose this to the counsellor, then I cannot overcome it. So, I feel let down and angry with the counsellor who cannot help me.'

This is particularly acute in those who are profoundly affected by shame and suffering from depression. The fear of revealing strong reactions, such as rage or tears, is a common problem in some depressions. The counsellor might ask him or herself questions such as:

- Has the person been punished in the past for revealing strong emotions?
- Is the person angry with herself for having such feelings?
- Does crying make her feel inferior and worthless in the eyes of the counsellor?

Such questions particularly address issues in the self–other schema.[6] A client of mine always felt bad when she cried. 'I hate you to see me like this', she would say.

Gilbert suggests some ways of working with clients who are struggling with deep shame. It is difficult to work with because the process of counselling relies upon disclosure, and shame craves concealment. Sometimes shame is responsible for emotional avoidance, episodes or states of being that are 'too painful to think about'. Another indicator for the counsellor is a feeling of being stuck, or a certain prickliness about the client which stirs up feelings of being attacked.

If the counsellor can recognise that these belong to the shame–rage process, then fear of rejection, loneliness and rage can be interpreted as part of the shame experience. The counsellor can then convey to the client that he/she senses and is trying to understand their struggle to disclose and the strength of the risk that the client is trying to take. The counsellor can then try and make contact with the loneliness and emptiness of the client and, if the therapeutic relationship is good, then this can build a bridge to the shame issue itself.

Once the issue of shame has been understood by both client and counsellor, then the working alliance established might benefit from some shame-reducing work. The use of a two-chairs technique where the client's internal dialogue is spoken out can help to illuminate the inference chain. Imagery might be used to help the client welcome and support the inner angry and rejected child (can you place that child in your lap and comfort her?)[7]

Gilbert describes 'the black hole of shame',[8] and this is exactly the language used by one of my clients, who spoke of the black weight in her chest, an immovable mass of fears, guilt and self-disgust. When this feeling is powerfully present, often the client finds it impossible to speak, and wants to run from the room. Should the counsellor remain silent with the 'frozen' client, or should they intervene? I agree with Gilbert that the counsellor must use empathic awareness to decide when the silence is a space in which work is being done, and to intervene would be unhelpful, or when the client is lost in it. In this case the counsellor may need to do the work.

The black hole contains strong feelings of guilt or fear, worthlessness or disgust that are difficult to describe. However, the events or story about which the client is ashamed are much harder to disclose. It may be a history of sexual abuse, or a previous abortion, or some aspect of their body about which they feel utterly ashamed. The difficulty in talking about this results from fear that the counsellor will reject the client, and guilt from an internalised voice which threatens punishment should disclosure take place. Particularly in cases where the shame is related to sexual abuse, the abuser may have demanded secrecy from the abused child ('This is our little secret. You must not tell anyone'), or threatened punishment if the child disclosed the nature of the abuse ('If you tell anyone, the police will take you away', or, 'If you tell Mummy she will be cross and beat you').

Family members in abuse cases may have invoked shame to inhibit the child from revealing the abuse to others, including telling the child that it was his/her fault or even denying that it happened at all. In one case the mother had not only denied the abuse, but had accused her daughter of being disgusting/terrible even to think that her father could have done such a thing. 'The experience of being disbelieved can be a powerful inhibitor of sharing feelings in counselling and is associated with feelings of shame and guilt in revealing, and also disgust at self.'[9]

Careful and sensitive questioning by the counsellor, coupled with a good working relationship, and a discussion of the dynamics of shame itself, help the client to feel safe enough to reveal what has been hidden.

CHAPTER 7

Jesus and Shame

WE POSTPONED OUR exploration of Jesus and shame from the earlier parts of this study concerned with the biblical tradition. While the biblical literature is primarily concerned with the kinds of cultural shame that are much closer to those of contemporary 'shame cultures', Jesus' thinking appears closer to the individual experience of shame more familiar to Western sensibilities. He does not teach particularly on shame, although he rebukes those who would be ashamed of him, meaning those who lacked the courage to identify with him or bear witness to him. Rather, in his parable of the Prodigal Son, and in his dealings with, and healing of, three individuals filled with shame – Peter after his denial, the woman suffering from a haemorrhage and the sinful woman who anoints him at Simon the Pharisee's house – Jesus identifies the steps to integration and healing which I will discuss in a systematic way in a subsequent chapter, utilising particularly the metaphor of the face.

We began earlier with Jane's story. Here is another story, one with power to transform and heal. It is the juxtaposition of our stories, and those of our clients, with this great Story, that is the particular focus of this study.

Jesus is accused throughout his ministry of associating with people and places deemed shameful by the official religious culture. The immediate context for the parable of the prodigal and his brother we will look at later is the accusation that 'This fellow welcomes sinners and eats with them' (Luke 15:2), an accusation also recorded by Mark when Jesus calls Levi, the tax collector, to follow him (Mark 2:15–17). The story which encapsulates this most vividly is that of Zacchaeus, the rich tax collector whom Jesus singles out in Jericho for hospitality and welcome (Luke 19:1–10). Probably amongst the most despised people in the city, Zacchaeus has grown wealthy by exploiting and defrauding the taxpayers of Jericho by taking a cut from the tax he collected. While the dishonesty is readily condemned by the morality of his day, since the taxes are collected for the occupying power of Rome, there are a whole cluster of other reasons for Zacchaeus to feel ashamed: he has regular contact with the Gentile powers of Rome, works for them and colludes with them. He is the last person in Jericho that a 'good' teacher should have contact with.

Zacchaeus climbs a tree to get a better view of the prophet from Nazareth. I wonder if it is that simple. Perhaps the leaves of the sycamore tree also afford an opportunity to see, but not be seen, to hide. What goes through Zacchaeus' mind when Jesus stops underneath the tree must be speculation, but my guess is that the horror at being exposed in front of the large crowd of the unsympathetic taxpayers of Jericho is replaced by unlooked-for joy as he is accepted by Jesus, who invites himself to his home. He has been used to entertaining fellow 'sinners' and his Roman overlords, but to be the honoured host of this 'good' man is utterly unexpected. To be a guest at someone's home is to accept them and affirm them, or to approve of their lifestyle, and it is this acceptance by the one whom Zacchaeus expects to reject him that has such transforming power. He repents of the activities which are dishonest (v. 8) and is affirmed as a true member of the community, 'he too is a son of Abraham', with no longer any need to be ashamed. The view of the wider community is, however, not so generous. Luke records that the crowd grumble, 'He has gone to be the guest of one who is a sinner' (v. 7). This is tantamount to sharing in their sin.

It is this power of acceptance which characterises all of Jesus' encounters with the shameful.

Jesus and the Woman with a Haemorrhage

Luke 8:40–48

This woman had been sick for twelve years, and while we cannot be absolutely sure of her condition, it seems likely that the haemorrhaging is uterine, creating the effect of continuous menstruation. While any protracted loss of blood is likely to produce anaemia and general ill-health, this particular condition is fraught with personal and social shame. There is still something about menstruation, even in our liberal and sexually frank society, which is secretive, almost shameful. Despite advertisements in magazines and on television for towels and tampons, most women treat their period as something private, hidden. A hundred years ago it was still called 'the curse' by some, and was even more of an unmentionable topic in polite society. In cultures that are secretive about sex, feelings of shame about any sexual matter are never far away, and I presume this was the case in Jesus' day too.

However, there was a more significant element in Jewish culture concerning menstruation and religious law. For the seven days from the beginning of her period, a woman was considered unclean and impure (Lev. 15:19), and everything or everyone she touched became unclean too. There were similar constraints around those who had a discharge of blood for many days: 'all the days of the discharge she shall continue in uncleanness, as in the days of her impurity' (Lev. 15:25). This woman in the gospel story had been ritually unclean for twelve years: shunned and shut out of religious and social life.

In contrast with Jairus, the synagogue ruler who fell at Jesus' feet and asked him to his face to heal his daughter, the nameless woman approaches him surreptitiously, from behind, hidden, hoping that a touch of Jesus' clothes, the edge of his garment or the tassels of his shawl, will bring healing. Her hopes are fulfilled, but she finds she cannot remain hidden: the healing of shame requires some exposure.

Jesus knows something extraordinary has happened: he feels a draining of power in some way which is difficult to explain. Matthew's account (Matt. 9:22) does not mention this almost magical element, as if he is embarrassed by it, and instead has Jesus first confront the woman before bringing the healing. The earlier account in Mark, followed by Luke, sets a different scene. The crowd is jostling Jesus like a star in the middle of a crowd of fans. People are touching Jesus constantly, which is why Peter is astounded at Jesus' question, 'Who touched me?' 'Everyone is touching you, Lord!' In the woman's mind she is exposed already. If Jesus knows her healing has been successful, next will come the finger pointed at her. No wonder she comes trembling to own up to her story. Will Jesus be angry with her? Has she 'stolen' power from him, which will now require recompense? What will she do? For she has nothing left, having spent everything on ineffectual cures.

Despite the shame of her past condition and the means by which she gained her healing, she comes forward and tells her story. The anger she feared is entirely absent from Jesus' response. 'Daughter, your faith has made you well: go in peace' (v. 48). 'Go in peace', *shalom*, is more than a kind 'good-bye'. It denotes not only her physical healing, but also the restoration of her life in society. No longer will she be an object of shame, but she can live open and free. Jesus is available to her, accessible to her and accepting of her. Again, it seems the acceptance of her timid and secretive approach by Jesus breaks the chains of chronic shame.

Jesus and the Woman Caught in Adultery

John 7:53—8:11
The discovery of this woman, caught in the very act of adultery, must seem a godsend to those eager to confound Jesus, the radical rabbi from Nazareth. This will test his wisdom and authenticity as a prophet from God. The law requires

71

that such a woman is stoned to death, and if Jesus is to remain true to the law, then he must affirm this punishment. Apart from challenging the primacy of his compassion, this has political consequences, for the Roman occupation has imposed upon the Sanhedrin a prohibition on using capital punishment for any religious offence. If Jesus affirms the death penalty, then he brings himself into conflict with the Roman authorities. On the other hand, if he does not demand that penalty, he contradicts the law and reveals himself to be 'soft on sin', contradicting earlier statements about requiring a higher standard of holiness from his followers than from the religious teachers who opposed him. Their trap is set to embarrass him and show him to be morally lax.

This story is all about shame and guilt. The trap is set to shame Jesus, and of course the wretched woman herself is being publicly shamed in a most humiliating way, both by the exposure of an act which is by its nature private, and in this case, also immoral, and possibly also by her attire, or lack of it, as she is dragged mercilessly from the scene where she has been discovered *in flagrante*. There she stands, clothes dishevelled, hair loose, full of shame and terror.

Jesus averts his eyes and looks down at the ground where he is writing in the dust. He senses her shame, and also the shameless hypocrisy of her accusers. They demand a reply, and when he straightens up, he replies, 'Let anyone among you who is without sin be the first to throw a stone at her,' and then returns to his writings in the dust. John recalls how the crowd of vengeful accusers melts away, beginning with the elders (those who are principally testing Jesus), and the crowd which had gathered around, like schoolboys in a play-ground ready to chant 'Fight! fight! fight!' at the first sniff of trouble. Finally Jesus, still writing in the dust, is left alone with her, and he stands up again. 'Woman, where are they? Has no one condemned you?' he asks. 'No one sir.' 'Neither do I condemn you. Go your way, and from now on do not sin again.' Guilt is not an irrelevancy to Jesus (do not sin any more), but it is subordinated to the more powerful and potentially more destructive problem of shame. Both Jesus and the woman have been victims of the manipulations of the scribes and the Pharisees, experts in guilt. Both Jesus and the woman are set free by the wisdom of exposing the shame of hypocrisy. It is finally the self-righteous who go away with heads bowed, and the accused who leave heads held high. Jesus, stooping down and writing his gospel message of freedom from shame in the dust of our lives, knows that we need first and foremost to know we are accepted, rather than condemned, if we are to deal with our guilt.

Jesus and the Sinful Woman

Luke 7:36–50. Cf. Mark 14:19; John 12:1–8

There is a cluster of gospel stories about the anointing of Jesus by a woman at a meal. In Mark 14 the scene is the house of Simon the leper and the emphasis is upon the cost of the ointment used and the challenge to her profligacy by those who want to see this expensive resource used in charitable concern for the poor.

Luke's version of the anointing story is set in a Pharisee's house and the woman is a sinner who anoints Jesus while he reclines at table. The focus is upon the contrast between the neglect of his most basic hospitable duties by the Pharisee and the open, generous, erotic actions of this woman who has responded to the accepting love of Jesus.

The version in the Gospel of John has certain similarities. The setting is a dinner, but this is at the familiar home of Jesus' friends Martha, Mary and Lazarus. A woman anoints Jesus' feet with costly ointment (pure nard, used as perfume on special occasions), and is chided for her profligate use of this expensive perfume by Judas, who is concerned not just about the poor, according to the Gospel writer, but also about his own pocket, since he stole from the common purse which the disciples owned.

Thus, there are similarities between Mark and John. In both gospels the event takes place in Bethany, although at different houses. In both an alabaster box of nard is broken open and used to anoint Jesus, but in Mark it is used to anoint his head, while in John it is used to anoint his feet. In John the woman is Mary the sister of Martha, in Mark the woman is unnamed, and in both stories an argument ensues about the cost of the ointment and the possibility of it being sold and the proceeds used for charity. In both stories Jesus interprets the act of the woman as an anointing before burial, but only in Mark is the telling of the story as a remembrance of her foretold. I think that there are sufficient similarities between the two stories in Mark and John to suggest that they had their origins in the same event. However, there is a separate event recorded by Luke, some aspects of which have become conflated with the other gospel versions. For instance, in Mark the nard is used to anoint Jesus' head, as would be expected (nard was used as a perfume for hair), but the story in Luke has the woman anoint Jesus' feet, and this element has crept into John's version of the story, where Mary also anoints Jesus' feet and wipes them with her hair. This part of the story properly belongs to the separate event recorded in Luke, where the woman is designated a sinner. Neither the woman in Mark's account, nor Mary the sister of Martha in John's, are described as sinners.

Luke's account of a woman anointing Jesus is, therefore, a separate event, with no debate about charity, a hostile setting, a sinful woman and a parable about the cancelling of debts and the depth of gratitude and love. Whilst the stories in both Mark and John have their elements of conflict, if we presume that the mode of anointing in John is a gloss on the story imported from Luke's story, it is in Luke alone that a strong theme of shame is present. This version of the story is the one we will explore.

The story in Luke 7 is one of the most disturbing in the whole gospel narrative. Jesus has arrived at a village and preached at the synagogue. He is the exciting new rabbi from Galilee. Controversial, perhaps, but he is young and the religious mainstream still affords him some room for manoeuvre. But these things need to be tested, and by each of the argumentative, sectarian religious parties in turn, to see if 'he is one of us'. The politico-religious context in Jesus' day was riven by factions and sects, each considering themselves to be the true believers.

After the service, Jesus is invited to the home of the leading layman in the village, who is also an important figure in the synagogue. Luke introduces him as Simon the Pharisee. The meal to which Jesus is invited takes place in the open air, probably in a large courtyard, with guests sitting around a low table and reclining on one side to eat single-handed. This is no private affair, because in such leading and wealthy households the conspicuous display of riches is made by the lavish provision of food, and the whole community gathers to sit or stand around the edge of the courtyard and listen to the conversation.

Imagine the rumours that run around the crowd when Jesus is not afforded the common courtesies of the time. Any guest in Simon's house would expect to have their feet washed by a male servant, their head anointed with a little oil and to be greeted with a kiss by their host. Simon has done none of these, perhaps because he disapproves of Jesus' teaching in the synagogue, and Jesus is publicly humiliated by his host.

Among those watching around the edge of the courtyard is a woman of dubious morality. Some traditions have described her as a prostitute, while others have seen her as Mary Magdalene making her entrance into the story of Jesus' disciples. She is clearly known as a sinner. She has come prepared to express her devotion to this new teacher, perhaps because having heard him preach she has already become captivated by his accepting love, and experienced something of the forgiveness of God which he proclaims. She is sitting

behind Jesus and is so upset by the way that Simon has mis-
treated Jesus that she cannot help herself. She begins to weep
and her tears fall on Jesus' feet. A stunned silence falls around
the courtyard. How embarrassing, how shameful. Why
cannot she control herself? However, it gets worse. Not content to let her tears fall on his feet, she lets down her hair and
wipes them away, even as more fall. No woman let her hair
down in public: such a provocative sexual gesture was for
husbands alone, or for the clients of women such as her.
Remember how deeply controlled dress and behaviour were
in Jesus' day. This is a shocking and provocative gesture by a
woman who seems to have no shame, but who in fact is consumed by shame. Her shamelessness is a cover for her
shame-filled life. So she wipes his feet with her hair. Only
male servants wiped men's feet, and never with their hair.
The question is, what will Jesus do, how will he respond?

He could have played it safe and save face by reprimand-
ing the woman, pushing her away and invoking the customs
of the day, shaming her more. This might have won the
approval of the Pharisee, and certainly of all those decent folk
of the village, not least the womenfolk whose husbands
might be tempted by her charms. Surely, he knows what sort
of person she is, says Simon.

Or he could have responded to this blatant sexual advance
as any red-blooded man might. Yes, ignore it now, of course,
but later . . . She has little reputation to defend and it is her
way of being grateful – take advantage of both her and the
opportunity.

But what Jesus actually does is shocking, not just because
he refuses to shame her further, but in criticising his host, he
invites others to regard him as someone who is himself
shameful. He identifies with her, not the moral cultural
norms. In so doing, his actions and words take away the
depth of shame that is internal so that she cares less about the
social shame, which continues. Rather than saving face, in a
culture consumed with doing the right thing, where saving

face is crucial, Jesus saves the woman. He is not ashamed of her, and by not being ashamed he demonstrates his love for her: not the abusive lust of other men, but the love under control, the saving love, the love which puts the other first, the love of God himself.

Jesus contrasts her unselfconscious and lavish response to the mean-minded response of Simon and concludes with the one thing guaranteed to really upset the Pharisee. He forgives her sin, something God alone can do. He demonstrates he is at ease with his sexuality and hers, because it is not out of control. Her physical intimacy, rather than being a contributing factor to her inner shame, seems to be a means of reducing it. What had been kept hidden, her tears and shame, is exposed, and healed by the accepting love of Jesus.

Peter's Denial and Restoration

Matthew 26:69–75; Mark 14:66–72; Luke 22:54–62;
John 18:15–27; 21:15–19

At the Last Supper Jesus had predicted that Peter would deny him (Luke 22:31–34). After the arrest in the Garden of Gethsemane, Peter's trial of his faithfulness to Jesus takes place as Jesus is examined before the High Priest. The gospel writers' intentions are to contrast the faithfulness of Jesus with the faithlessness of Peter. Jesus passes the test, Peter fails it.

Peter follows Jesus at a distance, with another disciple, probably the same disciple as the one whom John calls 'the disciple whom Jesus loved'. This may have been John himself. Luke and Matthew follow Mark's account, which is the gospel which relies most upon Peter's own testimony, and refer only to Peter. However, John's account is also close to Mark's, and so all four gospel writers are agreed on the broad sweep of this narrative.

Peter has followed Jesus to the High Priest's house where the trial is to begin. It is cold and Peter is both frightened and curious. He wants to 'see how this would end' (Matt. 26:58) So he goes into the courtyard where others are gathered around a charcoal fire and in the flickering light a servant recognises him as one of the disciples. Aware that Jesus' life is in danger, and that he risks guilt by association, he denies knowing Jesus. Another person emphasises the accusation that he is one of those associated with the accused. 'Man, I am not' is Peter's heated reply. A third person identifies Peter. The synoptic gospels leave him nameless, but John identifies him as a relative of the High Priest's servant Malchus, who had his ear severed by Peter's blow. This is getting very difficult, for Peter has been recognised by his face and by his distinctive Galilean accent. With curses and an oath, according to Matthew, Peter says 'I do not know the man!' This third denial is immediately followed by the crowing of the cock, and Jesus turns to look at Peter. The memory of Jesus' words, his own proud boast that he would die for Jesus and the craven way in which he has failed even to admit to knowing him trigger the affect shame. It is as if he has been kicked in the stomach. The shame runs deep and he leaves the scene of his failure weeping bitterly. Under pressure, his courage has failed him.

There is a pattern to this in Peter's life. In the boat on the stormy sea it is Peter who is bold enough to step onto the waves, but whose human resources fail to match the challenge (Matt. 14:22–33). It is Peter who both correctly identifies the true nature of Jesus' identity with the acclamation 'You are the Christ, the Son of the Living God', then completely misunderstands what that means (Matt. 16:13–20). Who knows how many times he had bitten off more than he could chew and repeated the pattern of shameful failure?

Peter leaves the scene of the Passion a broken man, but it is Jesus' gentle restoration of Peter on the beach at the Sea of Tiberias that once again demonstrates how Jesus deals with shame. The absence of any direct rebuke is striking. All that is needed are three questions about Peter's love for him to match the three denials. Each question, met with an affirmation of Peter's love, reveals the tasks for the restored disciple. "'Simon, son of John, do you love me more than these?" He said to him, "Yes, Lord, you know that I love you." Jesus said to him, "Feed my lambs"' (John 21:15). The 'more than these' probably refers to the other disciples rather than the fishing gear to which Peter had returned earlier that day. Peter had claimed pre-eminence amongst the disciples, a position he was to assume after Pentecost, but here at this moment is a broken man who can only affirm his love for Jesus rather than engage in arrogant comparisons with the others. The old Peter might have done, pointing out that he and the other disciple alone had followed Jesus to the trial, all the others having fled. Earlier in the gospel narratives we meet a Peter who is responding to shame with a narcissistic self-sufficiency. The Peter we meet after his denial is more honest with himself about his shame, and so on the road to restoration. Jesus' acceptance of him and his gentle but firm therapy of questioning and approval allows Peter to be restored.

The reason we have explored these incidents in Jesus' dealings with others struggling with shame is simple. If, as I will argue next, one of the important spiritual resources for those who want to escape from chronic, toxic shame is an encounter with Jesus, we ought to know what kind of response they will meet if they are to encounter Jesus Christ through prayer and reflection. Will it amplify the shame, ignore it, or heal it? I believe that shame is alleviated by encounters with Christ and that therefore, the church of Christ, if it is to follow in the way of Christ, should be a community which is honest about shame, recognises it and finds ways of healing it. Sadly, much of the life of the church only serves to amplify shame or positively create it in the first place. Or else it ignores it, preferring to deal in the currency of guilt and forgiveness, which is dealt with in easier, less costly and more mechanical ways.

The Parable of the Prodigal and His Brother

Luke 15:1–32

I must confess a prejudice here. This is my favourite parable and the one that for me above all else defines in parabolic terms the character of God. Having said that, it does deal in the experience of healing shame, and so to close this chapter by looking at this parable of two lost sons is not mere indulgence on my part.

The context for this parable is the familiar accusation that Jesus is shameful in his associates (Luke 15:1–2: 'This man welcomes sinners'). Jesus challenges conventional religion, and Luke in his gospel is often at pains to show how Jesus is a friend of the social and religious outcast, from the shepherds (first-century 'wide boys' and a byword for sharp practice) to the lepers healed (5:12) and the criminal on the cross (23:40). This parable is firmly in the tradition of shocking counter-intuitive religion.

There are two halves to this parable, the losing of the younger son (vv. 11–24) and the losing of the older (vv. 25–30), and its formal structure is that of a drama in four acts.

1. The division of the estate

The younger son asks the unthinkable. He is really saying 'I want you dead' in the Palestinian culture of Jesus' day.[1] The request for his share in his father's estate is so shocking that even today it would be unthinkable to ask this of a Middle Eastern father. In granting the request, the father shows unbelievable tolerance and love, whilst the older son demonstrates how out-of-relationship he is with the family. In the culture of the day, he would be expected to take his father's part and rebuke his younger brother, yet he remains strangely quiet. Today we would describe this as a deeply dysfunctional family.

What everyone would have expected the story to say would be that the father, on hearing the request, disowns his son and blesses the older brother. But so great is this father's love that he even allows for the freedom of his son to reject him. How like God! . . . and how unlike our expectations of him!

The son leaves in haste, no doubt because, as the story spread around the community, it becomes increasingly hostile to this younger brother, until he is almost fleeing for his life.

2. Into the far country

Wild living (here, there is no mention of immorality – that is the older son's unfounded suspicion – just wastefulness and profligacy) means that the younger son soon spends his share of the inheritance. Then a famine comes: without money, and with a sudden shortage of friends, he faces starvation. He hires himself out for work, and even agrees to work for a farmer who raises the unclean stock, pigs. He still has no food, however, and so he comes to his senses, but note what he wants: employment, but not relationship, and certainly not dependence in any way deeper than the provision of the means to avoid destitution. 'Here am I starving to death, and even hired hands back home have enough to eat. I will arise and go to my father and say to him, "Father, I have sinned against heaven and against you. I am no longer worthy to be called your son; treat me like one of your hired hands."' He has not yet realised that the fundamental problem is broken relationship. He does not yet have a sense of shame.

He rehearses this all the way home! He still wants to be independent, just as we do. We think that a little religion might not be too bad, but God wants us to live in utter dependence upon his love and grace. The root of sin is broken relationship, unwillingness to trust and the desire to live independently of God. So we get to the end of our own resources and promise that we will live better lives, go to church, anything reasonable as we bargain with God. But we fundamentally misunderstand our predicament, which is one of profoundly broken relationship with God, a brokenness we are powerless to remake by ourselves.

3. The homecoming

The younger son's problem is not only with his father, but also with the village, and the father's actions are best understood as a calculated attempt to shield his son from the anger of the village and the dangers of the lynch mob. Eastern gentlemen do not run anywhere, yet this father runs to greet his son. The response expected by Jesus' listeners is one of rebuke, yet this father greets his lost son only with hospitality and love.

Note the son only says part of his speech. He leaves off the end phrase, 'treat me like one of your hired hands'. In the face of such extraordinary and outrageous love and forgiveness, he sees himself as he truly is, and now he wants not a job, but a restoration of relationship. He has repented of the real problem, the real sin, the true heart of all sinfulness: the selfish, blind independence of spirit which says 'I did it my way.' At the moment he sees his true shame he also sees the welcome which dissipates it.

So, the son is home, the fatted calf is killed, he wears a new ring and robe and slippers are on his feet, and everything seems to be fine as the village shares in the celebration, now that the wider community is enabled to follow the lead of the generous father.

4. The older son

He has been at home all this time, seething with resentment. But this show of outrageous love is too much. He publicly humiliates his father by refusing to go into the feast and play the part expected of him, the older brother. He shows that in his seeming obedience he has actually been a slave, deprived of spiritual freedom all along. Look at the exchange between older son and father.

'You never gave me so much as a young goat, a kid, to have a party with my friends.'

'But all that I have had is yours, you received your share too when your brother left for the Far Country.'

'Yes, but I do not have the right to do with it what I want, I am not free to dispose of it. I own everything, but can use nothing.'

'O, I see, you too want me dead . . .'

Out and out rebellion is perhaps not the most dangerous kind of broken relationship after all. To live in the father's house with the heart of a sullen slave is more dangerous still, for it remains hidden until perhaps too late. The younger son was truly guilty of shameful behaviour, but the older son was perhaps the more inwardly shame-filled.

In the face-to-face meeting with the unexpected and outrageous love of this father, the younger son finds forgiveness, restitution and a new life. More than he deserved, certainly, but no more than the grace of God offers. His shameful and wilful actions at the start of the parable, driven by who knows what personal psychological crises in this atypical Palestinian family, are healed by the acceptance of the father. It is in such unlooked-for acceptance by God and his people that much shame is healed. The trouble is receiving it when shame so deeply shuts a person off from the contact which might just break open their defences and give them hope. The other trouble is that Christian people are as afflicted with as much shame as the rest of humanity, sometimes more, and find it hard to be as generous-spirited as God.

⋙

Shame: A Cure?

THE CONDITION OF shame has its origins in both the personal history of the individual, their inner psychological world, and the wider social environment of relationships. Since chronic shame can afflict whole societies, such as the exploited and the vanquished cultures of the Weimar Republic in post-First World War Germany or the Palestinian communities of the West Bank and Gaza Strip in contemporary Palestine, addressing only the personal psychology of the shamed individual will prove inadequate to the task at the macro level. Social and political policies are needed. Pattison approaches this theme as he explores the ways of dealing with shame in the second half of his chapter on the task of integration.[1]

I am reluctant to talk about a 'cure' for shame, because it sounds too final, and the most we might be able to expect in many cases is an alleviation of the worst effects of chronic shame. I share Pattison's sense of the difficulty of the task

The condition of chronic shame is a hard one to ameliorate because individually and socially alienated people are, by definition, fundamentally cut off from the individuals and communities who might help them. With defences against further humiliation and rejection in place, any attempts to build interpersonal or social bridges may themselves be perceived and treated as threats to any sense of personhood and self-respect that an individual may still possess. Thus attempts to enhance integration may at best be futile, and at worst may reinforce shame.[2]

The first step must be recognising that shame is a

major component in a person's want of wholeness. This is followed by a choice of three broad approaches: self-help, accompanied-therapeutic and ritual-spiritual. Self-help approaches take the form of book-based or group-based programmes, such as John Bradshaw's *Healing the Shame that Binds You.*[3] These approaches require a degree of hope and personal self-esteem which is likely to be beyond the ability of those most affected by toxic shame, and the attempt to secure a cure by such means, if met by failure, is almost bound to leave the unfortunate worse off than before, with even greater despair and self-loathing for their personal failure.

Accompanied therapy is the means by which the individual seeks help from a professional therapist or counsellor to alleviate the chronic shame. The theoretical backgrounds to the therapies are varied and the approaches legion, but the distinguishing feature here lies in the fact of a companion helping the shamed person. We shall explore some of the therapies and some of the personal qualities required of the therapist if effective help is to be offered.

Thirdly, and perhaps in conjunction with either self-help or accompanied approaches, are a number of religious or spiritual approaches to shame and here I will draw from my own Christian faith perspective to suggest an approach which helps to deal with toxic shame.

Identifying Shame

There are difficulties even in identifying shame, for it can easily be masked as depression or grief. In addition, shame by its nature wants to hide, and the presence of shame may be so painful that the person effectively defends him or herself against it and is unaware that shame is deeply rooted. Sufferers may present as depressed, but medication will only continue to mask the condition. A question to be asked of those who do not respond to normal treatments for

depression is 'how much does shame contribute to this condition?' Given the continuing stigma attached to mental
health problems in British society, many people suffering
from depression will feel a certain amount of shame, but if it
is not simply the sense of personal failure that often accom-
panies those who succumb to any form of neurosis, its roots
may lie deep in the childhood of the individual.

Amongst the physical indicators of shame are the same
signs, or vestiges of the signs, of shame in the infant: averted
gaze, downcast eyes, blushing. But in the adult these signs
may be well masked. The inability to articulate the feelings
linked to shame, or a general inability to speak, might indi-
cate its presence. The person may want the therapist to look
away, or leave the room, and the person may avert their own
eyes and avoid eye contact with the therapist.

When the person can speak, then clues include words that
express feelings of worthlessness, lostness, failure, rejection,
stupidity and inadequacy. Feelings are often spoken of
metaphorically, or by means of visual images such as 'a black
hole in the heart of me' or descriptions of feeling small and
lost in some dark or open place.

Once shame is acknowledged by the person there is not the
same immediate owning of it as in, for instance, previously
unacknowledged anger. The work of uncovering shame is
slow and painstaking, and must not be rushed, nor should
there be a search for some easy or quick fix.

Accompanied Approaches

Whenever an individual seeks help from another person,
rather than attempting to approach the problem on their
own, the dynamic of interpersonal relationships immediately emerges. The journey towards wholeness is now
undertaken in the presence of a companion who exercises
more or less direction in the pace of the journey and the route
it takes. Some approaches might seem little more than accom-

panied self-help programmes, whilst others can seem more like an abuse of power and overt control and manipulation of the client by an over-ambitious therapist.

The first step, as we have seen, is for shame to be acknowledged by the client, and it is generally agreed that this can be difficult. The very act of seeking help can itself exacerbate a person's sense of shame, with feelings of inadequacy and failure attached to the need to seek help from a therapist. Self-help approaches may well have been explored before, and if accompanied by a sense of failure, this amplifies the hope-lessness attached to the next step of seeking help from a counsellor.

A client of mine needed constant reassurance that she was not wasting my time. Her own sense of worth was so low that she felt any help by another person would be a waste of their time. The counsellor must avoid any signs of boredom with the client, for they will be very sensitive to any hint that they are unwanted. This is hard to do if the material is very repeti-tive, or the counsellor has had a late night!

The counsellor must also avoid seeming disinterested. On one occasion, around a break in the counselling due to a holi-day, a client came ready to disclose a significant part of her story, a step of great difficulty for her. Insufficiently attuned on that occasion (I am sure there have been many others too), I came across to her as distant and disinterested, hooking into her shame and convincing her I was not genuinely interested in her. She did not disclose that part of her story on that occa-sion, and it took many months to undo the breach of trust involved.

The requirements on the part of the therapist are not dissimilar to those required for many other conditions clients seek help for. There needs to be a safe environment, both physically and emotionally, to enable trust to grow. This may well take much longer than usual, especially if the root cause is some profound breach of trust on the part of a significant adult in the childhood story of the person afflicted with toxic shame.

The person with a self shaped by shame will have to find new ways of making sense of their life, ways not dominated by the low self-image associated with shame. The loss of this old perspective and the finding of a new one is a long and difficult process, with many points of 'shipwreck' on the way. Close attention, faithfulness, genuine interest and perhaps even love for one's client (in the sense of a desire to seek their well-being above the personal costs of being their companion on the way to wholeness) are essential. This opens up a minefield of transferential dynamics, with some clients' initial idealisation of the therapist never being overcome. Others feel that the constraints of the counselling contract signify a lack of real concern by the counsellor, who is only available to the client on the limited basis of the weekly session. Some therapists have advocated that for those with chronic shame the strict adherence by the counsellor to the contracted hour should be relaxed, and a (nonetheless professional) relationship that attempts a more equal basis, with the counsellor available to the client outside of the agreed sessions, should be adopted.

There appears to be more confidence that shame might be identified than that it can be 'cured'. Even the identification of shame is fraught with problems, since the very exposure of the condition, which by its nature is hidden, can drive it deeper into the defended self. The consensus of opinion, expounded above, is that the usual psychotherapeutic dynamics apply, and that with good-quality therapeutic help, the condition responds.

With the first condition required for a good working relationship being trust, some clients find it impossible to begin, with that trust too difficult to establish. However, when trust is established, then the gradual process of seeing in the counsellor a condition of unconditional trustworthiness and belief in the client, accompanied by patient listening to feelings and content, can allow the client to mirror that response in their own self-belief and self-image, and change from seeing themselves as victimised or faulty to acceptable and good enough.

However, it may well be that something more is called for, something that authentic Christian faith might offer in its contemplation of the life of Christ, symbolised by his face, and in the steady acceptance by a trusting community, alongside the kind of careful and lengthy therapeutic work suggested already. This particular contribution, derived from all that we have said about Jesus and shamed individuals in the previous chapter, will be explored in greater depth in later chapters looking at the face and mirrored glory.

CHAPTER 9

Shame and the Face

CROUCHED, HEAD BOWED, fingers covering the eyes, palms covering the cheeks, elbows tight to the body: shame covers its expression behind a mask so that the face becomes hidden. The face is a key to both the condition and the cure for acute shame.

Hiding the Face

First, a story. Ovid gives the classic formulation of the myth of Narcissus, a story about a face. Ted Hughes has retold it with revelatory power.[1] The water nymph Echo loves Narcissus, but he spurns her,

> But when she emerged from the undergrowth
> Her expression pleading,
> Her arms raised to embrace him,
> Narcissus turned and ran.
> 'No', he cried 'no, I would sooner be dead
> Than let you touch me.' Echo collapsed in sobs,
> As her voice lurched among the mountains:
> 'Touch me, touch me, touch me, touch me.'

Echo wastes away until all that is left is her voice repeating the last word or two of whatever she hears.

Narcissus has rejected others beforehand, and Nemesis, 'the corrector', hears their pleas for vengeance. One day Narcissus comes to a pool, gazes at its mirror-like surface and falls in love with the face he sees in it, his own face. 'He could not believe the beauty/Of those eyes that gazed into his own.'

As Narcissus bends down to kiss the lips of this face, so it rises up to reciprocate, but at the moment when warm lips should meet his own, only cool water dissolving the image greets him. He does not recognise himself.

> He had chosen
> From all the faces he had ever seen
> Only his own. He was himself
> The torturer who now began his torture.

When at last he realises that this image is his own face, he longs for death, and so wastes away. When they come to cremate the body all they find is a flower of white petals surrounding an egg-yellow trumpet, the narcissus.

Many of the themes in the myth are echoed in the experience of narcissism and shame. Narcissus is born out of violence, as the nymph Liriope is raped by the river god Cephisus, who becomes an absent father. He remains ignorant of who he is and of his origins. The seer Tiresias pronounces before his birth that Narcissus will not know himself, and he becomes trapped in his inability to be self-aware. A narcissistic dimension is present in his aloof character and his spurning of the love of others. Perhaps behind this is a fear of being possessed (his cry to Echo of 'Do not touch me') or of exposing the vulnerability of needing another. Instead all he seems to need is himself.

Mollon notes that a motif of central importance is that of reflection and illusion. Echo's cries are an auditory reflection of what she hears Narcissus say. She cannot take the initiative in speaking to Narcissus, only repeat the last two words or so of his own speech. This is paralleled by the scene at the pool, where Narcissus becomes captivated by his own reflection. He does not recognise himself and is in love with an illusion. If we see his image as a metaphor for his own self, his own soul, then he has the terrible fate of reaching for his own self, only to find it is unreachable and that he can never be integrated. The result of this self-absorption and self-lostness is death.[2]

Self-Awareness

At about eighteen months old, children become self-aware. Before this stage of development, a child looking in a mirror sees another child and looks behind the mirror to find it. The connection between the self and the image of his or her own face is not yet present. In a sense, the child is a stranger to itself. But as the brain grows, so the child becomes aware that he or she is a person, with an identity, recognisable in a mirror: 'This is my face, this is me.' This development is matched by a growing awareness of the identity and needs of those who are not 'me'. To a greater or lesser extent the child develops empathy, the ability to see and respond to the needs of others. When an adult, say their mother, is hurt (perhaps by shutting a finger in a door) an empathic child will want to replay what has been offered to him or her on many occasions of bumps and bruises, and 'kiss it better', or give the adult a cuddle. When self-awareness and empathy are twisted or limited in the growing child, then issues of narcissism and shame are not far away.

Narcissistic Disturbance

Shame is closely related to narcissistic disturbance, where the empathic response is absent or limited, and the individual becomes self-absorbed, interpreting the world only through the lens of their own needs. It is as if they have fallen in love with themselves. A common criticism of the narcissistic is that 'they only love themselves'. Shame is related to this because the person who is suffering from chronic shame becomes painfully aware of their own lack of worth and shortcomings, and compensates either by withdrawal from others (the drive to hide) or by using others to meet their needs (narcissism).

Shame, the Body and Sexuality

While the face is the focus of the hiddenness of shame, the rest of the body itself is closely related to shameful feelings, especially the sexual areas. In a woman the body posture that I described at the beginning, crouched, head bowed, arms covering upper torso and hands the face, precisely covers the more sexually freighted parts of the body. The crouch hides the genitals, the arms the breasts, the hands the lips, mouth and eyes. Shame and sexuality are clearly linked, not least in the Genesis myth, where awareness of sexuality is linked to being ashamed. In German, the terms for the sexual areas are explicitly linked to shame. The genital region is called *die Scham*, the pubic mound *Schamberg* and pubic hair *Schamhaare*.

The developmental origins of this might lie in the look of alarm on the mother's face when a child explores its genitals,[3] the look of disapproval and alarm being one of the first narcissistic injuries. What is pleasurable becomes forbidden and shameful. As in the Genesis myth, sexuality leads one out of the Garden of Eden. This is in contrast to the look of affirmation on the mother's face in her acceptance of the child. Wurmser states:

> Love resides in the face – in its beauty, in the music of the voice, in the warmth of the eye. Love is proved by the face, and so is unloveability proved by seeing and hearing, by being seen and heard. A child can be loved without being given the nipple, but love cannot exist without face and music.[4]

Whatever the origins of the shame response, the area of sexuality is replete with elements to reinforce the shame. The act of sexual intercourse between parents is generally hidden from the child, who experiences embarrassment on the faces of the parents if they are 'caught in the act'. The discovery that the genital organs in the opposite sex are different is fascinating for the child, but the discovery can be associated with rebuke from parents and shaming. Later, the sexually aware and active teenager is bombarded in our culture with images of the perfect body (interestingly, the size-8 female body familiar in many models and so beloved of girls is less attractive to boys than the pneumatic 38D breasts of the lad-mag, a torso which is pretty much anatomically impossible on a size-8 body!). Most teenagers do not have the perfect body of the advertising industry, be it the super-thin girl or the 'six-pack' chest of the male model. These perceived deficiencies can result in intense feelings of shame about body-image at a time when feeling physically attractive to potential sexual partners is important. Particularly acute are observations about the face. Is the nose too large, too thin, too squat? Lips too thin, eyes too close? And many, of course, suffer the embarrassment of acne. If the media speaks of 'cheek-bones to die for', the shame of the less than perfect face can give rise to shame which vulnerable young people do die for.

Revealing the Face

The face, this object of wonder, loathing, window on the soul, revealer of emotions and significant aspect of our identity, is hidden with shame. Could the uncovering of the face play its part in the reduction of shame-distress?

The role of the empathic counsellor

As we saw in the previous chapter, the counselling process aims to work sensitively to allow the story about which the client feels acute shame to be told. Empathy, patience, under-standing and careful questioning that demonstrates that we understand the risks involved all help the client to begin to trust that they can risk a verbal uncovering or unmasking with the counsellor. This might be accompanied by the physical uncovering of the face by the hands. This work cannot be forced, or hurried. The client will disclose when he or she is ready, and not before. The basic qualities in the counsellor of genuineness, self-disregard, non-possessive warmth and trustfulness (we might translate those into the more familiar categories of Christian virtue, honesty, selflessness, love and faithfulness) are vital if sufficient trust is to be built in order for the client to risk disclosure. Particularly with shame, the fear of rejection by the counsellor is strong, affirming for the client all the messages of worthlessness and self-disgust which they play on an internal tape-loop of inner speech. The counsellor's refusal to reject might be one of the key elements in rebuilding a sense of self-worth in the client. It is as if another story, contrary to the one they habitually play, is being experienced.

As the client risks disclosure, so the fear of rejection becomes acute, but the experience of welcome and acceptance by the counsellor contradicts this fear. If acceptance, welcome and hospitality of soul are all aspects of the broader category of love, then it is no surprise that the Scriptures have noted its power in dispelling fear. 'There is no fear in love, but perfect love casts out fear; for fear has to do with punishment, and whoever fears has not reached perfection in love' (1 John 4:18).

This is the necessary experience of acceptance in the counselling process. However, I think there are two other dimensions to the face which amplify and consolidate this experience of acceptance: meditating upon the image of the face of Christ and participating in a community which rejects condemning and judging as modes of control, and lives instead by accepting love.

The face of Christ

In 2 Corinthians Paul speaks of the glory of God seen in the face of Christ, and I believe that one starting point for reducing excessive shame is the contemplation of the face of Christ, both metaphorically and, through the medium of the icon, in some ways in actuality. It is in relationship to the gracious acceptance of Christ, taking us as we are, that a fundamental healing begins. Here, maybe, is one of the roles in which Christian art truly excels, having a deeper impact than the much more familiar wordy way of conveying Christian truth.

One of the obvious aspects of the face of Christ is the absence of any record of how it actually appeared. By the time of the Renaissance, artistic convention dictated that this face should be bearded and the hair worn long. From the majestic figures of Christ in glory found in Burgundian apse paintings of the eleventh century, through the long era of the Gothic, with Giotto (1266–1337), to the earliest stirrings of the Renaissance in Fra Angelico (1395–1455), the structures of the convention became fixed. The hair is worn long and parted in the centre, the skin is pale and the beard brown. Most follow the convention, with Piero della Francesca's (1450–92) *The Baptism of Christ* and Hieronymus Bosch's (1474–1516) *The Crowning with Thorns* being southern and northern European examples respectively. One notable exception is the Florentine Sandro Botticelli (1445–1510) whose *Pietà* of c.1490 has a shaven Christ in the arms of his mother. This figure is almost blemish-free, the suffering seen less in the dead body of Jesus than in the faces of those who witness the scene. This figure of Christ has more in common with the eroticised figure of Mars in his well-known *Venus and Mars* of c.1480.

So we *think* we know what Jesus looked like, and that is something akin to Robert Powell in the film *Jesus of Nazareth*. Everyone in medieval Europe thought they knew, at least. The roots of this artistic convention could be found in the two 'true-likeness' traditions of the Veronica and the Mandylion of Edessa. The Veronica was assumed to be the miraculous representation of the face of Christ on the cloth offered by St Veronica to Jesus as he carried his cross. A play on the word Veronica is *vera icon* meaning 'true image'. This became the most famous relic in Rome and was reproduced everywhere: it showed a full-frontal face with sad eyes, a long, slender nose, shoulder-length hair and a beard. Lost in the Sack of Rome in 1527, it was as venerated then as the Shroud of Turin is today.

The East had its Mandylion of Edessa, with images in Paris, Genoa and Rome each claiming to be the genuine article. This was one of a number of miraculous images of Christ supposedly not made by human hand which appeared in sixth-century Byzantium, and they too follow the physiognomic conventions.

The probability is that the Veronica, the Mandylion and Turin Shroud are all thirteenth-century forgeries, which leaves us with as good a guess at the true likeness as anybody. We are free to imagine the features of Jesus and to impose a look which tells us more than simply the arrangement of his eyes, nose and mouth. This is exactly what Bosch has done in *The Crowning with Thorns* and another example of this is the artist who, painting in the workshop of Jan Mostaert from Haalem in the 1520s, was influenced by the *Devotio Moderna* and produced a picture designed to elicit from us our compassion and contrition (*Christ as the Man of Sorrows*). But what defines the limits of our imagined face and whatever is projected onto it? The defining limits should be theological not imaginative. It must be the portrayal of the character of God revealed in Christ, imprinted upon the blank canvas of the face of Christ.

The visual component is matched by the theological. Jesus Christ is the opposite of the narcissistic self-absorption of the shame-filled. His face looks towards God and others, and in our facing of him lies the possibility of transformation.

David Ford in *Self and Salvation*[5] reminds us that the face of the risen Christ disturbs ordinary recognisability.

> The risen face of Jesus is a 'revelation' not in the sense of making him plain in a straightforward manner. Rather, what is 'unveiled' is a face that transcends simple recognisability, that eludes our categories and stretches our capacities in the way which God does. It provokes fear, bewilderment, doubt, joy and amazement . . . It generates a community whose life before this face is endlessly interrogative, and whose response to it leads into ever new complexities, ambiguities, joys and sufferings.

Again and again it is the hope of seeing the face of Christ which is the eschatological climax. It is the vision of Christ seen by John on Patmos, and the hope expressed by Paul in 1 Corinthians 13:12 that while 'now we see, in a mirror, dimly, but then we will see face to face. Now, I know only in part; then I will know fully, even as I have been fully known.'

This face is deliberately unrecorded in its historical particularities, for it expresses the glory of God, as Paul asserts in the following passage:

> . . . all of us, with unveiled faces, seeing the glory of the Lord as though reflected in a mirror, are being transformed into the same image from one degree of glory to another . . . For it is the God who said, 'Let light shine out of darkness,' who has shone in our hearts to give the light of the knowledge of the glory of God in the face of Jesus Christ.
>
> (2 Cor. 3:18, 4:6)

Yet, for all of its potential to embrace the fullness of the breadth of God, this face does have historic particularities. It is a Semitic face, and it becomes a wounded and bruised face, with a brow pierced by deep puncture wounds from a crown of thorns. The witness of the New Testament and the gospels in particular gives a story and context to this face which reveals God's glory, and more precisely, gives shape to our understanding of the nature of God as revealed in this face. The orientation of this face towards God in faithful obedience, and towards others in self-giving compassion and acceptance, has a particular resonance with the condition of shame. It is as we recognise in the loving gaze of Christ the full acceptance of God that we find the courage to face our shame, and it is in his responsive orientation towards the well-being of others that we discover the antidote to the toxins of narcissistic self-absorption and self-loathing that can distort healthy shame into its malignant variant, destructive shame.

An Accepting Community

The healing of shame comes from acceptance of who we are, and in the pastoral life of the church that is expressed in Eucharist and fellowship. The pastoral task here is to allow such dimensions of community to develop that we are able to give expression to our deepest longings and fears without rejection by others, or such acute embarrassment and shame that we turn away. Prayer is one way of expressing those deep places, praise another, and a tender embrace another. There is a longing for churches where prayer can be poured out, praise offered in extravagance and love shared that does not abuse others or reinforce shame. The pastoral leader has a special responsibility to foster such communities, in the hope that the Christian church might point to a better way of living than is common in the shamelessness and shame-filled-ness of postmodern culture.

In the Eucharist we are faced by others. In the peace we greet and face the other. In receiving the cup, we are faced by the one who serves us. All this shapes a *habitus* of facing. Above all, it orientates us to the face of Christ. This is symbolised in some Eastern traditions by the great icons of Christ in majesty in the apse above the altar, or in Western traditions by the Crucified One. It might be the icon before which we encounter Christ, or probably, just the Christ we configure in our mind's eye. Similarly, in baptismal practices, we face Christ. 'Do you turn to Christ?' the candidate is asked, or 'Will you follow Christ?' We face up to our old sinful past, and face Christ.

But in every case, the face of Christ is immediately seen in the faces of others. The 'do this' of the synoptic gospels is echoed in the example that Jesus gives in John's Gospel of washing the disciple's feet. To face Christ is to wash feet, die to live, take up a cross and live compassionately and joyfully for others. To see this face of Christ as we share in the Eucharist meal is to see a face alive with the life and glory of God, open to all that is new and orientated towards others. This face of Jesus Christ is so directed towards others that knowing and loving this face means being called to know and love them and to recognise this face in theirs. As James Fowler puts it so succinctly, 'Grace – the grace of God and the grace mediated through the love and acceptance of humans – is the antidote to and the healing power for shame.'[6]

This can all sound hopelessly naive and idealistic. In reality, within Christian communities we can often encounter narrow-minded bigotry, hypocrisy and a culture which is shame-inducing rather than shame-reducing. Pattison notes that:

> the relationship between shame and Christianity thought and practice is complex and ambivalent . . . Christianity can create, exploit and deny shame in groups and individuals. However, it can also diminish and alleviate shame, enhancing worth, efficacy and esteem.[7]

Those versions of Christianity which over-emphasise the sinfulness and utter worthlessness of humanity can easily play on the young and instil a sense of shame at simply living. Meanwhile sermons every Sunday that attempt to shame people into submission to a moral code too easily underline a sense of shame in those vulnerable to its manipulation.

What might be explained as simply the shortcomings of those self-styled proclaimers and teachers whose repertoire of didactic tools is limited to guilt and shame, and thus judged as merely the product of individual limitation, can take a more sinister turn when the church's outright oppression and denigration of marginalised groups is considered. The paternalistic theology which views women as less human, and more sinful, than men is an obvious structural source of shame (and this despite the evidence that men contribute far more to the sum of human misery than women), as is the exclusion of those whose sexuality is deemed heterodox (homosexuals and bisexuals). If history is written by the victors, then such theological shaming is clearly written by the powerful as a means of maintaining their grip upon power. These attitudes of manipulation and control echo more closely with the voice of the pharisees who Jesus condemns than with voice of the Son of God.

The Christian church, if it is to be a community which alleviates shame rather than arousing it, needs to take a careful look at the practices whereby it seeks to ensure conformity of behaviour and attitude on the part of its adherents. The issue is complicated by the ambiguity which lies at the heart of the faith. The acceptance by God of the sinner, no matter how heinous his/her sin, is not an excuse for licence. Real, deep and lasting change of character and behaviour is a hallmark of authentic discipleship. However, whether shame-inducing and guilt-arousing methods of ensuring such radical change are effective is debatable. In the Christian faith, the means of ensuring an outcome are as important as the outcome itself, and 'the end never justifies the means'.

Equally important to the practices of social control are the images and metaphors from which the community derives its meaning, and especially its view of the God whom it seeks to

worship and follow. The postmodern suspicion of all knowledge as a bid for power might actually be of help here, if it
enables the church to distance itself from the prevalent concept of God as simply monarch, lord or sovereign. Feminist
theologians have long argued that such dominant metaphors
are the product of a male-dominated church, allied to political power which in the post-Constantinian era required a
God to match the absolute rule of the Emperor. The absolute
power of this God becomes matched to the authority of the
monarch, state or church, despite the contradictions to power
and control explicit in the teaching and life of Jesus Christ. In
the Kingdom of Heaven power is a very strange commodity,
wielded by those who serve, rather than by those who rule,
by those who lay down their lives rather than by those who
seek to maintain them.

The picture of the kind of deity that emerges from the early
Christian communities which created, for instance, the Christ
Hymn of Philippians 2:5–11, is distinctly different.

> Let the same mind be in you that was in Christ Jesus
> who, though he was in the form of God,
> did not regard equality with God as something to be
>   exploited,
> but emptied himself,
> taking the form of a slave,
> being born in human likeness.
> And being found in human form,
> he humbled himself
> and became obedient to the point of death
> even death on a cross.

By contrast to what one might expect of an Eastern, despotic
monarch, the revelation of the character and nature of God
seen in the person of Jesus Christ is not exploitative or
manipulative, but self-giving, emptying himself or being
poured out for others (the Greek word *kenosis* can be
translated variously). Despite the notorious difficulties in

translating and exegeting this passage,[8] it certainly cannot be used to create a God who holds onto power and exploits it to his own advantage. Clearly, this image of the self-emptying God is in Paul's mind as he encourages the Philippians to imitate the humility of Christ:

> Do nothing from selfish ambition or conceit, but in humility regard others as better than yourselves. Let each of you look not to your own interests, but to the interests of others. Let the same mind . . .
>
> (Phil. 2:3–5)

If we allow the earliest Christian traditions to determine our understanding of God revealed in Jesus of Nazareth, then the picture that emerges is one that is radically different from the normal pattern of human will to power. It has to be said that it is also different from the image of God portrayed in some sections of the Old Testament canon, who appears to exploit shame as perversely as any despot. His people disobey him, and he covers them in shame. Shame and dishonour are still powerful cultural shapers in Eastern societies, as we have seen earlier, and it comes as no surprise to see the same values written onto the character of God in the Old Testament. However, the church, while holding the Old Testament as Holy Scripture, is called to follow Jesus Christ, who radicalises the Jewish faith of his day and whose revelation of God both fulfils and contradicts some Old Testament themes. When sections of the church seem to prioritise the Old Testament over the New in its portrayal of God, it is often to highlight the shaming actions of God: to emphasise his wrath over his love, his judgement over his mercy.

The image of God that we derive from the life and teaching of Jesus includes some themes from the existing Old Testament theology. The wicked are punished, God is holy and human sinfulness defiles the person who commits it. But, particularly in the parables, we also see a God who forgives outrageously, who loves and gives people freedom and who in Christ is not distant, but present.

Pattison describes a series of images about God which he believes exacerbate the elements of humiliation, inferiority, unloveableness and unwantedness that characterise shame: images such as God's being wholly different to human beings, his disembodied state, his purity and holiness, goodness and perfection, his passionlessness, omnipotence and absence. The God he describes does not need anything from us, but sees all everywhere. There is no escape from the eye of this God, before whom we are exposed in all our shame. This God, he argues, leaves us in a state of 'almost permanent chronic shame and abjection'.[9]

He is powerfully attractive to the narcissistic, the shamed and the wounded, but does not heal their shame. There are kinds of beliefs implicit in parenting that produce shame-filled children and adults, for example:

- that respect for parents is due whatever their actions, rather than earned through care and nurture
- that children should be disregarded simply because they are children
- that tenderness is harmful
- that pride and arrogance is dispelled by fostering low self-esteem (never praise a child, always disapprove)
- that the body is disgusting and dirty
- that emotional coldness prepares a child for the knocks of life.

Some of these beliefs seem dangerously close to beliefs in this kind of Christianity. When we conceive of God treating us like this, he affirms abusive parenting and guarantees the validity of actions that create shame.

However, this God seems distant from the God of Jesus Christ. The problem with the church's image of God is that it is not sufficiently shaped by Jesus Christ, but is independent of him. In such ways, it is more prone to being merely our own abusive and controlling beliefs and actions, written large upon the heavens.

The God revealed in Christ, however, is not distant, but present with us and takes human form, with all that means in terms of embodied existence. Jesus of Nazareth was truly a human being, who needed to eat and defecate, who had sexual desires and possessed genitals. He laughed – not the condemning laughter of the Old Testament God who in the face of his enemies laughs at them ('you hold all the nations in derision' [Psalm 59:8]) – but the warm-hearted rejoicing over good (Luke 10:21). He accepts the unclean, unwelcomed and shameful and embraces them. If the Christian God is a shame-inducing monster (a projection of male narcissism) then it is precisely because this is not the God revealed in Christ, and the church has failed to proclaim the true character and nature of God. It has become Deist and not properly Christian.

What might a Christian message that disarms the power of shame look like?

It would first replace the monarchical, traditional God, so obsessed with guilt and punishment, with the God who loves and cares. Certainly, we should not ignore the holiness and perfection of God, but the idea that all he seems to be interested in is the failings of individuals needs to be challenged. God is concerned with the recreation of all things, human beings included. That recreation is part of the replacement of sinful, evil and destructive systems with the Kingdom of God, full of peace, justice, righteousness and joy. In that Kingdom there will be no shame.

The reality of the distorted character of every human life needs to be told alongside the good news that every human life matters, is loved infinitely, is of glorious worth in God's eyes and is the object of God's saving purposes. God does not just judge the sinner, but he also loves the sinner. The longing in God's heart for the best for all gives rise to the need for repentance, for we must not proclaim a message that says, 'do not worry what you do, or how you live, for God loves you and doesn't mind evil and wretchedness'. That would undermine the primacy of God's love, for love desires the best in the other, and so God calls human beings to turn away from all that destroys and violates.

The demonstration of that loving commitment to human well-being and renewal is seen with greatest clarity in the death of Christ:

> God's love was revealed among us in this way: God sent his only Son into the world so that we might live through him. In this is love, not that we loved God but that he loved us and sent his Son to be the atoning sacrifice for our sins. Beloved, since God loved us so much, we also ought to love one another.
>
> (1 John 4:9–11)

So, it is here that we look for the images that can reduce our sense of shame. Here, we must distinguish between guilt and shame. In the death of Christ God has identified with our sin, so that we can be forgiven and our guilt taken away. Here also, the true worth of God's beloved creatures is seen. Perhaps we might listen to the inference chain derived from the monarchical view of God.

- God is all powerful, pure and holy, and he despises sin.
- Humans are sinful, and so God judges and rejects them.
- I am human, and sinful, so God rejects me.
- He turns his face away from me in my sinfulness.
- Any sense of self-worth I have is actually pride, and pride is the foremost of all sins, so I should view myself as worthless if I am to be acceptable to God.

The response of Christianity rooted in the loving incarnation of the Son of God in Jesus of Nazareth would be thus.

- God is almighty and pure, and he despises sin and all that harms his creation.
- Humans are sinful, but they are also the objects of God's love and care.
- I am sinful, but also loved and accepted by God through Jesus Christ.
- I have great value in God's eyes, and his face is turned towards me in longing for my best.
- Pride in my own self-determination, separate from God, is wrong, and this arrogant pride is harmful to me, but a sense of my own worth as God's creature is vital if I am to grow up in Christ. Humility must be distinguished from humiliation.
- Instead of hiding my face in shame, God wants me to look into his face with confidence in his acceptance and love for his care.

This is the significance of the face of Christ.

The community gathered around this story of God's acceptance is all too commonly marred by a spirit of rejection, exclusivity and judgementalism. As I have argued elsewhere, the pastoral task of creating authentic community requires the building of trust, fostering of friendship and a realisation of what that community embodies.[10] The Baptist Union of Great Britain adopted Five Core Values in 1998 as a response to a call to shape a denomination committed to the poor and marginalised and issues of equal opportunities. One of those values was *An Inclusive Community*, called to be like Jesus in his welcoming attitude to everyone. It remains to be seen how committed the Baptists (and I am one of them) are to this value, but if it is allowed to find its expression in pastoral practice, then we might find ways of avoiding the judging/rejecting mode of being church, so concerned to maintain the purity of the community and defend its boundaries, and truly become an inclusive community.

In such a community, shaming is not used as a means of

social control (for instance, in enforced public confession of failings) nor is a person's standing in the community determined by age, gender, sexuality, social status, wealth or occupation. Children are not shaped by fear or guilt, but encouraged to develop their potential within the security of a caring community. Here the vulnerable and the shame-filled can find acceptance on their terms.

CHAPTER 10

Mirrored Glory: A Biblical Exploration

2 Corinthians 3

The image of the face, both the hidden face of the shamed and the contemplation of the face of Christ, has been central to our theological exploration of shame. We now turn to a more detailed consideration of the central scriptural passage in our analysis, 2 Corinthians 3.

This third chapter of Paul's second Epistle to the church in Corinth is all about glory. Its meaning is not immediately clear, giving rise to much speculation,[1] but at the risk of hanging too much significance on a disputed passage, I will argue that it points precisely to the two theological motifs that I have argued are central to the alleviation of chronic shame, openness to others and contemplation of the face of Christ.

Is the chapter about shame, though? Apart from the story of Moses' shame at his fading glory (a story which we shall see is itself dubious), this is not obviously a passage of pastoral guidance about the problem of chronic shame. We need to remember that the current understanding of shame is a Western, and not an Eastern one. Shame functions differently in those cultures where honour and shaming are commonly used as a means of social control, and we ought not to be surprised if the New Testament does not directly address some of the concerns that trouble postmodern, Western and twenty-first-century society.

However, if we remember that the opposite of glory could well be something like shame, then this chapter has indeed a great deal to say about this matter. Elsewhere in the New

Testament Paul speaks of the long hair of a woman as her 'glory' (δοξα, *doxa*), while if a man has long hair it is a 'disgrace' (ατιμια, *atimia*) or 'shame'. Glory and shame seem to function as antonyms.

The conclusion which Paul draws from his tortuous arguments about the Old Covenant and the New is that 'all of us' are 'being transformed into the same image from one degree of glory to another' (v. 18), a transformation from shame to glory. The larger purpose of the section of this letter in which chapter 3 appears, a section which begins in 2:14 and concludes in 6:13, is a defence of the particular style of Paul's apostolic ministry. It is a ministry of sincerity (2:17) and glory (3:8–11), of boldness (3:12) and hope. Paul argues that he does not need letters of recommendation to substantiate his ministry, because the Corinthian Christians themselves are his letter, not written with ink, but in the Spirit.

Paul's defence of the character of his ministry includes as one important feature the demonstration that the human weaknesses and frailties which characterise it do not undermine its credibility but, on the contrary, reveal precisely its Christ-like character (4:7–12, 16–18, 6:3–10).[2]

The New Covenant is being contrasted with that derived from Moses, the Old Covenant. The Old is of the letter (its origins in the chiselled letters on the Sinai tablets) as opposed to the New which is of the Spirit (v. 6); it kills and leads to death, even if its origins were marked by glory (v. 7) and it condemns rather than justifies (v. 9).

Paul's purpose in this argument is to establish that his ministry possesses *doxa*, glory. His opponents, presumably, are keen to establish how shameful his supposed credentials are. He is an itinerant preacher with a prison record and not fit to be an apostle of the Lord of glory, they claim. However, Paul wants to establish that by contrast with the glory of the New Covenant, of which he is an apostle, the Old has no glory at all. This is why Paul introduces the story of the veil over Moses' face. Some explanations of this story argue that

Moses' glory began to fade, and that the veil, originally in place to spare the eyes of the Israelites, remained in place long after it was necessary, because Moses was ashamed of it departing. It is this version with which we opened the introductory chapter.

This version, however, has been disputed. Hays[3] points out that if the Exodus story depicts the glory on Moses' face as fading over time, then Paul has 'at hand an obvious symbol for the impermanence and obsolescence of the old Mosaic covenant'. However, Exodus 34 neither uses the verb καταργειν, *katargein* (fading) nor says anything about a fading glory in the story. Some argue that Paul must have been working from an established midrashic tradition (a tradition of commentating upon the Torah) but there is no direct evidence that there exists any such midrashic tradition (indeed later rabbinic traditions explicitly state that the glory did not fade).

There is an alternative explanation. The verb so often translated 'fading', *katargein*, does not mean to fade, but rather to nullify, to invalidate or to render ineffectual. It is used by Paul elsewhere to mean precisely that (Gal. 3:17, Rom. 3:31, 1 Cor. 2:6). Paul means that the glory evident on Moses' face, the glory of the Old Covenant, was a glory that in Christ has been superseded and is now nullified. It is Paul's retrospective theological judgement. The NRSV translation is correct:

> Now if the ministry of death, chiselled in letters on stone tablets, came in glory so that the people of Israel could not gaze at Moses' face because of the glory of his face, *a glory now set aside*, how much more will the ministry of the Spirit come in glory? . . . not like Moses, who put a veil over his face to keep the people of Israel from gazing at the end of the glory *that was being set aside*. (vv. 7–8, 13)

while the NIV translation incorrectly opts for the older view:

111

the Israelites could not look steadily at the face of Moses because of its glory, *fading though it was* . . . We are not like Moses, who would put a veil over his face to keep the Israelites from gazing at it while *the radiance was fading away.*

It was not the end (τελο, *stelos*) of the glory that was hidden from the Israelites, in the sense of its departure, but rather the purpose. So, Moses' veil was in place to prevent the Israelites from seeing the true aim of this passing covenant (although quite why that should be so is, again, much debated). Paul is arguing that if the veil over Moses' face was there to prevent the Israelites from seeing clearly its true aim, then by contrast, the New Covenant, of which Paul is the apostle, is illuminating rather than obfuscating. The veil is removed and glory revealed. Hays exegetes this as follows:

> The veil on Moses' face hid from Israel the glory of God, which Moses beheld at Sinai, a glory that transfigured him. Israel could not bear looking at the transfigured person and concentrated instead on the script that he gave them. That text, too, bears witness (in a more indirect or filtered manner) to the glory, to the person transfigured in the image of God, who is the true aim of the old covenant. For those who are fixated on the text as an end in itself, however, the text remains veiled. But those who turn to the Lord are enabled to see through the text to its *telos*, its true aim. For them, the veil is removed, so that they, like Moses, are transfigured by the glory of God into the image of Jesus Christ, to whom Moses and the Law had always, in veiled fashion, pointed.[4]

It is in Christ that glory is experienced, and shame removed. Those who live by the shaming scripts of past failures, shortcomings and trauma, find the veil remains over their lives. They live veiled to the true freedom of living openly and gloriously. But how does this transformation take place?

112

We turn to v. 18, the climax of Paul's argument. Paul does not need to veil the glory of the gospel of Christ; he does not need to hide its true purpose and character, because where the Spirit of the Lord is, there is freedom (v. 17), that is, freedom to speak the gospel openly and boldly (v. 12). The appropriate manner for ministering the new covenant is openness, while the appropriate manner of conveying the old is a veil: the new is written in human lives, the old in letters on stone. Paul is continuing to contrast the old and new covenants.

So, with unveiled faces, we (that is those in Christ) see the glory of God, as in a mirror. The question this raises is, what is the mirror? Most would argue that the mirror (κατοπτρίζομαι, *katoptrizomai*), which reflects the glory of God, is the life and character of Christ, symbolised by his face. It is in Christ that we see the glory of the Lord, as in a mirror. This is later echoed in v. 6:

> For it is the God who said, 'Let light shine out of dark-ness,' who has shone in our hearts to give the light of the knowledge of the glory of God in the face of Jesus Christ.

However, Wright argues that the mirror in which we see reflected the glory of God is one another:

> At the climax of Paul's whole argument, he makes (if I am right) the astonishing claim that those who belong to the new covenant are being changed by the Spirit into the glory of the Lord: when they come face to face with one another they are beholding, as in a mirror, the glory itself . . . It is the peculiar glory of the Spirit that is seen when one looks at one's fellow Christians.[5]

Mirrors in the ancient world were generally polished metal, which gradually tarnished and clouded the image they were reflecting. To avoid this, constant polishing was required, with elbow grease being more in evidence than metal polish! To reflect the glory of Christ needs constant attention. The same could be said of the need to be aware of the corroding action of our postmodern culture, with its tendency to exacerbate shame. The picture is not of a quick glance in the mirror, but a continual gaze, with attention to the mirror's surface. To counter shame's toxic effects requires regular attention, a repeated look into the face of Christ, and a repeated vulnerable openness in relation to others. Or to change the metaphor, a repeated listening to the gospel story about Jesus of Nazareth and regular and repeated engagement with the liturgical and communal life of the church (provided that the church community itself is not responsible for increasing toxic shame, as we noted earlier). This suggests that reducing toxic, chronic shame is not a simple, one-off exercise, but rather inculcating habits of a life-time. Those advocates of a pastoral or prayer-ministry exercise in removing shame that is either quickly accomplished or easy to conclude are surely misguided. There is no quick fix for chronic shame, only the steady gaze at the Christ who accepts us and a life spent with those who share that vision.

So there is a process of transformation taking place, which is the work of the Spirit, a process of being transformed from shame to glory, from hiddenness to openness, a process which takes place when we see the image of Christ reflected in others. It is both the contemplation of the particular glory of Christ, a glory seen in suffering as much as in triumph and etched upon his face, and that glory reflected in the faces of those who follow him, who have learnt to remain vulnerable and open despite their shame, and thus found the toxicity of shame alleviated. They too interpret suffering, not as shameful but as, rather, imitating the glory of Christ, and thus full of glory.

Our two modes of dealing with toxic shame, contemplation of the face of Christ as a metaphor for living before the presence of God, and living openly and vulnerably with others who share that life, is expressed here at the climax of Paul's argument in v. 18.

The glory into which Christians are being changed, seen in an honest and open-faced friendship, is indeed seen in the face of Jesus Christ first. It is a glory which shines through suffering and everything which induces shame in us. This true glory is in the heart, rather than visible on the face, like the glory of Moses. It is the glory of a transformed life with its shame taken away. The power of the gospel story gradually, as it is boldly told, transforms the story of shame and humiliation into the story of glory.

CHAPTER 11

Jane's Story Continued

IN CHAPTER TWO we began to tell Jane's story. We pick up the story now as she enters counselling for what appeared on the surface to be depression, with chronic self-harm, accompanied by feelings of guilt and worthlessness.

A local network of Christian counsellors provided a directory of Christian counsellors, and Fran was a member, offering counselling by a Christian, without it necessarily being 'Christian counselling'. It was Jane's minister who helped her find a counsellor through the network, and so it was that one Wednesday evening Jane knocked on Fran's door.

Fran's approach to pastoral counselling was eclectic, but with a great emphasis upon a person-centred approach. Some years previously she had gradually explored counselling from her experience in her local church of being part of a prayer counselling team. A course in listening skills had followed, by which time she was keen to train as a pastoral counsellor. Four years of training had provided a firm basis for her practice, which remained informed by her Christian faith, but not explicitly, so far as her clients were concerned. More than half were in fact women and men of little or no committed Christian faith, yet they found in Fran a woman of genuine concern, reliability, wisdom and professionalism.

That initial hour with Fran provided Jane with some necessary information. Fran described her practice, confirmed that she subscribed to the British Association of Counselling and Psychotherapy Code of Ethics and that she was regularly discussing her work and clients with a more experienced counsellor who supervised her work, a universal practice amongst professional counsellors. Jane and Fran negotiated a suitable fee level, should Jane decide to see Fran as her counsellor, and Fran offered to Jane an initial contract of six sessions of fifty minutes each, should she decide to enter into a counselling relationship with her. Thursday evenings seemed to suit them both, and a tentative first booking was made for three weeks' time. They parted with this offer of a working relationship made.

More importantly for Jane, she left with an overwhelming sense that she had been listened to. She had not needed to somehow defend herself from the charges of failure as a Christian because she was depressed. Fran just accepted her for who she was. This seemed utterly remarkable to Jane, and left her with a curious mixture of fear, anxiety and relief. In the sleepless hours of that night Jane weighed the pros and cons. If she did nothing and turned away, would she be missing an opportunity to recover from the feelings of worthlessness and despair that sometimes overwhelmed her (she was now in a good enough phase to begin even to think about this: four weeks earlier she had been feeling much worse) and get herself together? But what would she find out? What would her friends think . . . and curiously, even though he was dead, what would her father think? Her mother, she was convinced, would disapprove.

In the morning, she had made up her mind to pursue counselling with Fran. After all, it was only six sessions, and she could stop whenever she wanted. A phone call that evening confirmed the first session's time and duration. However, her anxiety grew over the days and became a dull and pervasive sense of dread, punctuated at times by acute panic. This was not going to be easy for Jane.

The room Jane entered in Fran's home was no different to the one she had sat in during the previous exploratory interview. Two chairs were positioned at a 45° angle to each other, the one Jane sat in facing the door. A coffee table held a vase of flowers and a box of tissues, and the walls were bare except for a rather non-descript country scene of cows in a field. It was a calm room, if bland. It said little about its owner.

Fran chatted about the journey and the unusually warm weather for spring, then with a deliberate change into counselling mode, asked Jane about the feelings of depression. Jane talked about work, home, her church, her friends: certainly more personal information than she would have otherwise divulged with a woman she had only met once before, but nothing too intimate until Fran asked about her doctor. Had she consulted her GP about the depression? No, Jane had not. She did not want to get a health record that said 'mental health problems', but in the ensuing discussion Fran, for once quite directive, convinced Jane that a health check was necessary. Illnesses like thyroid deficiency can sometimes masquerade as depression, and it was important that this was checked, and if necessary medication for the depression prescribed. Jane agreed to see her GP as soon as possible, although probably not before the next session in a week's time.

In fact Jane did not see her GP until ten days later, and it was not as disagreeable as she had thought it would be. Her local practice included a woman GP who had a reputation for being a good listener, and gave Jane twenty minutes to describe her symptoms: loss of self-esteem, tearfulness, at times dark despair with no obvious cause. Really, it was a relief to be under the care of a doctor, and she wondered why she had not consulted her earlier. A course of antidepressants was prescribed, with the warning that they would take two to three weeks before any noticeable lifting of mood was felt.

Before that doctor's appointment had been kept, Jane's second appointment with Fran occurred. With growing confidence in Fran's gentle listening and perceptive observations, which accurately reflected what Jane had disclosed, she began to talk about her childhood. Not too personal yet, with not much about feelings (that was way too scary) but the relationships were described, and her sense of alienation from her mother was alluded to. It was not until her fourth session that somehow the floodgates broke (was it partly that the antidepressants had lifted her mood sufficiently to enable her to touch these deeper feelings, or was it simply her growing trust in Fran?) and she spoke about her mother's rejection of her in detail, and then cried for five minutes.

The fifth session was more of the same, and was also the time to review the renewal of contract. Did Jane want to continue in counselling, and was Fran able to continue to provide it? The response was yes to both, with another six sessions agreed, and after that the possibility of an open-ended contract. By now Jane was in too deep to pull out so soon, although she never felt she was trapped by Fran, but rather found that at some stages in the journey she felt dependent upon the process, if not actually dependent upon Fran, for her survival.

In fact Jane continued to see Fran for two and a half years, two years of which were weekly appointments. Space prevents the detailed description of the sessions, but the process could be said to have fallen into four broad phases: disclosure, ownership, healing and resolution.

The first six months were spent largely in disclosure, as Jane not only told the story she remembered well, but also the parts of the story that had lain half-buried and half-remembered. She regularly railed against her mother's indifference and coldness towards her, and the sense of lost-ness and worthlessness she had felt, even as a small child. However, it took four months before she hinted at any sexual abuse. First, her sister's advances towards her when Jane was eleven and Emily fifteen, when Emily came into the bathroom when she was getting out of the bath and offered to dry her. Jane had been surprised by this offer, but felt unwilling to refuse. Emily had not just dried her back, but had also begun to touch her between her legs, at which Jane recoiled. Emily blushed, and left the room, but on other occasions later she had tried to touch her inappropriately. This went on until Emily was seventeen, when she found a partner of her own age with whom she began a sexual relationship and the abuse stopped. Jane had never told her mother, and her father was absent, so the story remained untold until Fran heard it.

Jane felt both enormous shame at telling this story, and some sense of relief that at last someone else knew and, more importantly, had not turned away in disgust. This was very surprising to Jane – Fran seemed to just accept this part of the story, as if she had known all along what had happened. Given her own overwhelming sense of disgust at herself, Jane found Fran's acceptance unnerving. However, even this disclosure did not change how she felt about sexual intimacy. While she had been celibate since her relationship with Robert, she felt continually dirty in a sexual way, and avoided touching herself anywhere that was erotic. Her dress continued to be an attempt to cover herself, to be asexual, uneroticised, yet she never felt clean.

Owning these feelings took her into the second phase of counselling, and uncovered a deeper and more destructive abuse than the lesbian abuse by her sister. Throughout the early months of counselling she continued to speak of her late father in warm and affectionate terms. Fran would recognise this as a split between the good father and the wicked mother, the accepting father and the rejecting mother. But then Jane began to feel angry with her father, and not just because he had left her when she was ten. She knew that there were half-remembered flashes of memory, a large man pressing on top of her, and her holding her breath as he touched her legs, but she could not remember who this was. She remembered his breath, though, smelling of what she later knew to be whisky, but then, just blankness.

She also became aware that she was angry with him for leaving her a second time, just when they had begun to have something in common, her law practice. She had cried at his funeral, but there was something about the loss which was also deeper than his death.

The process of coming to terms with her grief took months in the middle of the counselling, but the process was hindered by the growing realisation that the large man of her early memory was not her uncle but her father. She had feared that revelation, and wanted to disbelieve it, but it was an extraordinary conversation with her sister that broke the log-jam. They had never been close, but the break-up of Emily's long-term relationship with her partner Susan had brought Emily to Jane's door in rage, despair and vulnerability. Over endless cups of coffee they had talked as never before, Jane telling her about her depression and counselling (and demanding Emily's discretion about this: mother must not know). What blew Jane's defences was Emily's question, 'Did Dad touch you up too?' It seemed that, being older, Emily had remembered only too well a few episodes when their father had been drunk and had come into her room and abused her sexually. Too afraid to tell their mother (who would not have believed her anyway), she had never told anyone in the family, although she had suspected that Jane had suffered too.

This revelation from Emily unlocked those dark possibilities that had troubled Jane: the possibility that it had been her father who had abused her, the father whom she looked to for refuge from her mother's rages, the father whom she had placed high on a pedestal of adoration, despite his later absence. Careful to suggest that memories might be false in an awareness of false memory syndrome, Fran helped Jane to discover as best she could the reality behind the memory. The events began to trouble her dreams and the nightmares she had always suffered from periodically became acute. In a recurring nightmare her mother would be chasing her with a knife, and her father would catch her, only for relief to turn to horror as he locked her into a small, dark room where there was no escape from her mother's violence.

This period of disclosure and ownership was the hardest part of Jane's journey, and her depression and anxiety were particularly acute, so that Jane was barely functioning at work, and not at all in her social life. It took all her energy to get to work, complete the tasks she had and return home. The rest of life was bleak. The church provided her with extra support in the form of friends who looked in most days, provided her with food, which she sometimes ate, and took charge of domestic chores. For a month or so at its worst she actually stayed with an older couple who provided her with a bed and support. This involvement of her church later proved to be one of the most healing aspects of her recovery.

Through this dark period Jane saw her GP each month, and for a short six-week programme was referred to the local mental health unit where she took part in some Cognitive Behavioural Therapy. The sense in which different players in the process of Jane's support worked together was unusual, but welcome.

Later, Jane thought about the various strands in the recovery process. She had the support of a pastoral worker at church who took some care of Jane, the couple who cared for her and the friends who supported her, as well as the local GP and mental health services, but it was above all Fran's careful and compassionate work with her that helped. Fran proved to be utterly reliable, and it was only twice that Fran cancelled appointments: once when she had flu and once when her own mother was taken dangerously ill. Given the poverty of Jane's ability to trust others, this rebuilding of trust (actually there was precious little to be rebuilt) was crucial in Jane's emerging health.

Above all, the work with Fran uncovered the hidden roots of shame that needed to be removed. The sense of shame at not being wanted, of being rejected by her mother, abused by her father, ignored by her two older siblings and then abused by one of them, Emily, was profound. Her early experience of church as an adult only emphasised the shame, as it reinforced her sense of failure and guilt. But this was a guilt that remained untouched by confession or communion. This guilt was about who she was, not what she had done, and was much closer to shame than wrongdoing. It had remained covered because the church did not know how to deal with it, and it was only the crisis of unmanageable depression (itself a symptom of the deeper cause) that provided the key to unlocking it.

The shame itself was not explicitly addressed until quite late in the process. The steady reliability and unfailing acceptance of Fran, and of Jane's Christian community, were crucial. They refused to spiritualise the shame away, as if a brief prayer, no matter how well meant or sincerely prayed, might touch this profound sickness of the soul. But they never gave up on Jane, and lovingly accepted her throughout. Wise and knowledgeable pastors did not expect a quick fix and had the insight and patience to persevere, and Jane was fortunate in both her counsellor and her church. Many others find that this combination is rare.

A remarkable turning point came when Jane dreamed one night, not of violence, darkness or rape, but of seeing what she recognised as the face of Jesus. She had not been expecting this. In her estimation God was often a harsh task-master, not a loving companion or welcoming saviour. Yes, she knew in her mind that he was both these things, but that conviction never descended the two feet to her heart. She 'knew it' but she had not experienced it, nor could she imagine it. But that dream stayed with her vividly, so vividly that she later came to the belief that it was no ordinary dream but an encounter with Christ himself. The face was open, welcoming, with a flicker across the eyes that was not laughter, but sheer joy. Somehow she knew that this person just loved her unconditionally, with no reservations, no hidden agendas and no secret pay-offs waiting in the wings. This face was not manipulating her, but just accepted her as she was, broken, sullied, fearful and lost.

As Jane recounted the dream (or the vision, which might be nearer the truth), Fran affirmed its significance and suggested that Jane might want to find a picture of Jesus Christ that came closest to the image she retained in her mind's eye, and to use this to meditate upon the reality behind the image. It took a while to find the picture that helped Jane the most, but it soon became part of her devotions at the beginning of each day. It was the Christ whose face she had seen who had accompanied her throughout the journey of recovery, who was the hidden presence in Fran's counselling room, the numinous Other in between Fran and Jane, who now became personal to Jane as she came towards the close of the process.

The final phase of growing into and becoming a person who is experiencing sufficient wholeness continues to this day. Jane has now fallen in love and is married to Cliff, copes with work and can even sometimes be civil to her mother. She still suffers from time to time with depression, and will probably always be prone to this affliction, but life is okay. She is now an open-hearted person who is able to relate adequately to others and is no longer crippled by chronic shame, although she still gets embarrassed easily. She sees Emily from time to time, and they are not exactly close, but are friends. Jane accepts Emily and her new partner Anna, and is no longer judgemental in her approach to Emily's sexuality, although that brings her into conflict with the strongly held views of some in her church. Finding a measure of wholeness and the loss of shame has not solved everything for Jane, and it was no quick fix. However, what has grown is good and sufficient.

CHAPTER 12

Pastoral Practice in Reducing and Averting Shame

1. Creating Non-shaming Communities

The possibility of creating non-shaming communities addresses at least two different concerns within churches. The first is the struggle to be inclusive communities, where otherwise stigmatised and scapegoated people (such as non-heterosexuals or members of some ethnic minorities) find a place where they are not just tolerated, but rather positively welcomed. For a person who feels shamed by their race or sexuality, to discover a community where they are welcomed is a necessity alongside any personal therapeutic help they might find.

The hostility that the Windrush generation of Caribbean Christians felt in the more traditional churches in the 1950s and 1960s in England is a lasting stain upon the reputation of mainstream religion in Britain, and a major reason for their search for a more inclusive form of Christianity elsewhere, particularly in the Black Pentecostal churches that were established in reaction to that hostility. It has taken half a century to begin to address those divisive splits. Currently one of the presidents of Churches Together in England, Revd Esme Beswick, is black, as is the General Director of the Evangelical Alliance in the United Kingdom, Joel Edwards. Amongst the fastest-growing churches in Britain are some of the black-led churches in London and the West Midlands (both Afro-Caribbean and African in culture), so the sense of black churches being on the margins is now redundant. However, black ministers in otherwise white-majority churches, such as the Church of England or the Baptist Union, still feel overlooked, and this contributes to the social shame that can be pervasive amongst societies. Positive discrimination to establish role models for black ministers and members remains a possibility (there are now both Diocesan and Suffragan black Bishops, and Methodist District Chairs, but no black Senior Regional Ministers amongst the Baptists), but perhaps the reality that the church in England is increasingly black will have more significance than any other measure to remove any remaining stigma attached to being a black Christian in Britain.

The second concern in creating non-shaming communities lies more generally in the use of shame as a measure of social control within the teaching and discipline of the church. This is a danger especially within the more literalist expressions of Christianity, such as Conservative Evangelicalism and Catholicism, although it is not confined to them. While the teaching or practices of these churches are probably not the primary cause of the chronic shame that afflicts some Christians (the primary cause lying in poor parenting or abuse), nevertheless, an unhealthy obsession with confession of sins, a reductionist view of the human soul as overwhelmingly, or thoroughly evil, and a consistent diet of sermons that affirm how bad those listening are reinforces the already established shame, rather than contributing to its alleviation.

The message of Jesus, if properly understood, should release churches from being communities that reinforce shame, and empower them to become places where men and women find healing from shame and where they can grow in their self-esteem and sense of worth as fully human beings loved and restored by a God of grace.

2. The Therapeutic Task of Alleviating Chronic Shame

If the personal therapeutic work which I think is vital for wholeness is to be properly addressed, there needs to be greater awareness of the characteristics and pathology of shame amongst pastoral counsellors and carers. Resources of skill, time and energy need to be spent in working with the chronically shamed. Often counsellors understand much more about depression, substance dependency, relationship processes or early developmental difficulties than they do about shame, and this theme must be better addressed in training and in the formation processes of the counsellor.

3. Working with Parents to Avoid Shame

For churches struggling to find ways of connecting with the majority of people locally who form the three-quarters of the population who indicated on the 2001 census form that they were Christian (let alone the other quarter), offering ways of caring for the community is paramount.[1] The growth in the number of broken homes, and the cultural emphasis upon the primacy of caring for children, should have created an opportunity for many churches to offer parenting classes to the local community. Spun off the back of the hundreds of playgroups and toddler groups, or offered to those who come to the churches for infant baptism, a course offered at low or no cost (perhaps run by professional child care workers who understand something of child development and care) would help to foster a climate in which parenting without shaming could become more of the norm than it is already, while offering a bridge to the wider community that still thinks of the church as a shame-inducing institution.

The church might also develop support for those who find mirroring difficult (such as those suffering from post-natal depression) within their own congregations. Offering this to those who have only a distant and vague relationship to the church would probably prove difficult, since it implies a high level of trust at a time of great vulnerability. However, there might be possibilities through networks of pastoral carers related to Christian counsellors and agencies.

This all presupposes that in its childcare practices, the church itself avoids those that generate shame in the young. High levels of discipline in the current climate would quite properly be seen as abusive, but in its teaching of children, an over-emphasis upon sinfulness, or the unacceptability of the child to God without an explicit confession of faith in Christ, or even an emphasis upon the failings of human nature without a corresponding understanding of the grace of God and his unconditional love, could be construed as shaming. I am not arguing for a Rousseauian doctrine of the essential goodness of human nature, but for a proper balance between the possibilities for both good and ill in human responses. Children can be cruel, harsh and violent, not least to other children, and any notion that children are saintly is soon dismissed by their parents, if no one else, yet they are also capable of great affection, care and concern, and this is too easily missed in some theologies where the child is said to be essentially evil. When this is coupled with child-rearing strategies that aim to 'break the will' and instil a sullen conformity, shame is almost inevitably a result.

4. The Christian Church Must Refuse to Play the Fame Game

The church has not been immune to the culture of fame, so obviously a feature of the shame-inducing narcissism of our contemporary culture. The stories of the famous being converted owe more to wishful thinking than to reality, in some cases. This is not to say that we should decry the conversion of Jonathan Aitken, a former Conservative Government Minister convicted of perjury, through the Alpha course, or the earlier supposed conversion of the 'page three' glamour model, Samantha Fox. Nor should we ignore those others who are Christians and whose lives are lived to some extent in the public eye, such as Cliff Richard. However, sometimes the church comes dangerously close to endorsing the very culture of fame that is so destructive to many. A proper humility and sense of the equality and dignity of all, whatever their familiarity in the public eye, is called for.

Evangelicalism too often wants its heroes and trophies in a way that panders too much to the spirit of the age. It creates its 'well-known public speakers' who ply the pathetically small world of Evangelical conferences and holidays, the organisers of which use the fame of the speaker or musician to attract the (fee-paying) delegate or holidaymaker, and make the event financially viable. I wonder what Jesus Christ would make of it all?

5. The Power of Shame Amongst Those in Pastoral Leadership

It is often noted that amongst the most powerful tools of social control at the disposal of pastors are guilt and shame. The routine liturgical rehearsal of our guilt in confession (whether corporate or individual) is matched historically by the use of shame and exclusion for those who are not compliant. This ranges from the subtle (or not so subtle) sense of exclusion that a gay man might feel within an overwhelmingly heterosexual congregation which never addresses the question of the inclusion of homosexuals because it is afraid of discussing such 'unpleasant' issues, to the explicit exclusion from Communion (the ban) or even removal from membership of those who are deemed to be unrepentant (normally for sexual sins such as adultery) within the more fundamentalist sections of the church.

Where institutions are more concerned with their public image or perceived moral purity than with pastoral inclusion, the routine use of shame as a tool of control will be almost unconscious. The church that acts like this will, strangely, attract shamed people, who will be conforming and hard-working, craving the affirmation that comes from the leaders who exploit them, and receiving it provided they remain passive and obedient. Those who find themselves unable or unwilling to conform will find themselves excluded from approval by the wielders of ecclesial power, or even demonised with accusations of a 'critical spirit' or a demon of rebellion. Such abuses of power further damage already wounded people, and give rise to anxiety amongst the obedient 'sheep' that remain. Infantile or shamed people might produce congregations of unchallenging people, but such congregations are a travesty of the vibrant and human communities that churches ought to be. The exploitation of shame by church leaderships and clergy must be exposed if it is to be transformed.

Some of the reasons for these continuing abuses lies with the way in which pastors are often women and men who themselves need affirmation from others to meet deep psychological needs, and an unhealthy cycle of co-dependence is established between pastors and their needy flock. Christopher Perry[2] suggests that pastors are more prone than any other professional group to feelings of guilt, self-criticism and self-denigration. This is rooted in a 'helping personality'. Drawing on the work of Karen Horney and Hugh Eadie, the profile of the pathological helping personality breaks down into eight components:

1. idealised self-image: the appeal of love
2. guilt: self-hate and self-criticism
3. obsessive–compulsive characteristics
4. affective controls on sexuality and aggression
5. passivity, compliance and conformity
6. attempts to resolve the conflicts
7. intro-punitive hostility and self-hate
8. stress symptoms

Feeding the pressure to love and serve others is the fear of rejection and the shame of failure, and so to avoid those dangers, the pastor exudes warmth and love. With so much denial and repression taking place, sexual fantasies and impulses are problematic. Retreating into the study and pulpit, the pastor takes refuge in a series of pastoral relationships which generally avoid intimacy (but which have the dangerous potential to become sexual and abusive), but which continue to reap an abundant harvest of approval to sustain his ideal self-image.

> To cope with this array of conflicts, pastors tend either to withdraw into an excess of 'being', symbolised through meditation, study and fantasy, or else, they become rebellious and impulsive and enact aggression or sexual impulses in a destructive and self-destructive way, quite often inviting condemnation from parishioners and ecclesiastical authorities alike. The latter is simply a massive reinforcement of the pastor's tendency to punish himself and to turn his anger against himself.[3]

The roots of this pathology lie in an absence of approval and a presence of shaming in earlier life. Given such paucity of affirmation, constant reparative activity is necessary to bolster the fragile ego, and the resultant messianic tendency, which constantly seeks to meet everybody else's needs through a punishing work schedule, or else to manipulate others by using the mechanism so familiar to himself, shame.

Given that a disproportionate number of clergy fall into the category of the 'helping personality', meeting their own needs through the unlimited care they give to others, it might seem a rather hopeless case. The church doomed to remain a shaming culture through the kinds of leaders it self-selects. Hard-working clergy respond to the over-weaning demands of congregations that legitimise their pathology under the fantasy of 'the mission of Christ'. However, better selection processes, a stress upon the importance of self-awareness in clergy and a culture that sees a readiness to embrace therapy as a sign of growth rather than a symbol of failure, might help to redress some of those imbalances.

If many pastors are compulsive carers, others are 'vain, ambitious and highly sexed'[4] and may themselves be the products of 'shaming narcissistic wounding'. These pastors quickly become aggressive, bullying and predatory. The damage they can do is profound. Shamed individuals as well as shaming structures create dysfunctional communities. The more we become aware of these, the greater the possibility of change and transformation to more wholesome ways of relating and living.

Pattison is acutely aware that with all of its promise of healing and belonging, the church still finds delivering on that promise difficult. 'The church "talks dirty", but can it actually cleanse and heal?'[5] He fears that there is a reluctance to deliver because if people 'attain a state of adequate responsible personhood, worth and self-esteem, they might become non-conforming, independent and critical of the church community; they may fail to contribute to it, or even leave it'. While such communities of the shamed and immature do not constitute human wholeness, they do make compliant church members. I share this concern, but feel that probably as important a reason for churches failing to deliver lies in sheer ignorance and denial about the whole hidden issue of shame.

6. Recovering a Proper Sense of our Place in Time

Colin Gunton has shown how postmodernism, or late modernism as he would prefer to call it, has a reductionist view of time. The past and the future are compressed into the present moment. 'We live in a this-worldly culture. Our time and space and not some distant heaven is the important reality.'[6] He goes on to show how developed societies like those of the West, with homes filled with labour-saving devices to save time otherwise filled with drudgery, actually have less time for leisure than so-called undeveloped societies which are, in fact, more leisurely.

Irenaeus, in his concept of time, affirms the goodness of creation, including time. For him eternity is not some discontinuous world, distinct from that of space–time which we inhabit, but rather the perfecting of the created order. Christ recapitulates, sums up and perfects what is temporally fallen in the coming fullness of the Kingdom of God. Those who followed Irenaeus were not so careful to give due weight to the created order, and Origen, more sensitive to Platonic influences, strays towards Gnosticism in his devaluing of creation and time, while Augustine's baleful contribution on this issue, as in so much theology, continues to exert its damaging influence. In Augustine, the Manichaean never fully disappears, and his claim that 'we cannot rightly say that time is',[7] coupled with his view that all of history is equally fallen, and that the incarnation is not an event in the story of God happening in a particular time, but a timeless presence inserted into time, together create a theology that separates creation and redemption, lacks a proper understanding of the work of the Spirit in time and ultimately reduces the significance of time which modernity readily endorsed.

It is precisely this loss of a proper concept of time as God's good creation that Lasch sees as one of the roots of the self-obsession in narcissistic culture. A weakened concept of historical continuity (and a mistrust of the immediately preceding era as repressive) and fears about the future, in an age haunted by fears of nuclear war, world-wide terrorism and ecological disaster, creates a culture of the 'now' in which it makes sense to live only for the pleasures of the present moment. The past is 'old hat', the future we might not reach, so live for today. It is a culture of hedonism, which, as we have seen earlier, provokes a rise in the experience of shame and shamelessness. In evaluating how to live in the present, it is self-scrutiny that is important. Narcissistic man questions his degree of the self-fulfilment that contemporary culture supposes is the prime aim of life by considering his own needs, and whether they are being met within a particular marriage or relationship, for example.

> . . . the culture of subjectivity . . . threatens society with its inherent solipsism and individualism in a manner which can only further intensify the very social factors which sustain the underlying insecurity and pessimism which have given this narcissistic self-concern its momentum.[8]

If, rather than the unipolar, introverted attempt at self-knowledge which is so attractive in this narcissistic culture, with its therapies of self-fulfilment, the self is essentially and irreducibly relational, then true self-knowledge will come only in relationship to the other. Indeed, if self-knowledge is only realised in the self-forgetfulness of loving another, we have precisely the opposite to the self-regarding dismissal of another's love that is enshrined in the myth of Narcissus, who rejects Echo's love and instead falls in love only with himself.

> True knowledge of self is . . . irreducibly bipolar, that is relational, and must be so if the self is to be construed as 'person', that is, as a being which is . . . non-self-contained.[9]

As the African proverb puts it, 'a person is a person only because of others and on behalf of others.'

Indeed, the Christian emphasis is not on self-fulfilment and self-preservation, but on a giving away of the self in relationship to others and the Other. Jesus says that 'those who want to save their life will lose it, and those who lose their life for my sake, and for the sake of the gospel, will save it' (Mark 8:35).

7. A Renewed Interest and Devotion to the Face of Christ

If in place of the self-regard that lies at the heart of both the narcissist and the shamed there needs to be a redirected gaze, away from self to another, then to whom should this redirected gaze be addressed? The one true man, the one who perfectly lives his life for others, and ultimately expresses his divinity in laying down his life for others, must surely be the prime object. There may be others who so live a godly and saintly life that their story and image also warrant our interest, and that is at least in part what the cult of saints is all about, but we only find them of value insofar as their lives accord with that of Christ's. It is their Christ-likeness which attracts our interest in the first place, as objects of our devotion. It is not Mother Teresa's crotchety temper and impatience, but her selfless concern for the poorest of the poor on Calcutta's streets that demands our wonder and warrants our interest. It is that which is most Christ-like about her that enables her story to scratch away at our story with its inordinate sense of shame.

Where Catholic and Orthodox traditions have valued the visual image as an aid to devotion and personal transformation, Protestantism has often been iconoclastic, fearing the visual and celebrating the verbal. It is a Christianity of the Word. It has something in common here with the more fundamentalist forms of Islam, with their horror of anything that is image (with, no doubt, its roots in the reaction of Mohammed to the idolatry of his own culture). Similarly, the Israelites reacted to the idolatry of Canaanite religion with a prohibition on images of the divine enshrined in the commandment 'Thou shalt not make any graven image.'

In opposition to both Judaism and Islam, however, Christianity is an incarnational faith. God has taken human form, wears a human face, and becomes like (and yet unlike) humankind. We saw earlier the promise and challenges of

135

depicting the face of Jesus Christ, but we should not allow the challenges to rob us of the promise, especially if contemplation of the face of Christ and a steady re-orientation of life towards his life, has such wholesome potential for the shamed and shameless.

NOTES

Introduction

1. Exodus 34:29–35.
2. 2 Corinthians 3:13.
3. C. D. Schneider in his entry 'Shame' in Rodney J. Hunter (ed.), *Dictionary of Pastoral Care and Counselling* (Nashville: Abingdon Press, 1990), pp. 1160–63, distinguishes between being ashamed (disgraced) and the sense of shame (modesty or discretion): thus 'disgrace shame' and 'discretion shame'.
4. Nedarim, fol. 20a.
5. Stephanie Dowrick, *Forgiveness and Other Acts of Love* (London: The Women's Press, 1997).
6. James W. Fowler, *Faithful Change* (Nashville: Abingdon Press, 1996), pp. 92–3.
7. Including a Jungian approach: see Mario Jacoby, *Shame and the Origins of Self-esteem: A Jungian Approach* (London: Routledge, 1994).
8. Christopher Lasch, *The Culture of Narcissism: American Life in an Age of Diminishing Expectations* (New York: Norton, 1979).
9. Fowler, *Faithful Change*, p. 93.
10. Schneider, 'Shame', p. 1160.
11. c.f. D. Nathanson, *The Many Faces of Shame* (New York: Guildford Press, 1987); *Shame and Pride: Affect, Sex, and the Birth of the Self* (New York: Norton, 1992).
12. Robin Stockitt has begun to explore this theme in '"Love Bade Me Welcome; But My Soul Drew Back"' – Towards an Understanding of Shame', *Anvil* Vol. 15(2) (1998), pp. 111–19. See also David Ford, *Self and Salvation: Being Transformed* (Cambridge University Press, 1999).

1. The Experience of Shame

1. Depictions of these two frescos are widespread. For instance, James H. Beck, *Italian Renaissance Painting* (Köln: Konemann, 1999), pp. 126–7; 'The Masaccio' in *Florence* (Everyman Guide, 1993), p. 309.
2. *Rome* (Everyman Guide, 2nd edn, 1998), p. 228.

3. James W. Fowler, *Faithful Change* (Nashville: Abingdon Press, 1996), p. 138.

4. R. Stockitt, '"Love Bade Me Welcome; But My Soul Drew Back"' – Towards an Understanding of Shame', *Anvil* Vol. 15(2) (1998), p. 113.

5. D. Atkinson, *The Message of Ruth: The Wings of Refuge* (Leicester: InterVarsity Press, 1983).

3. The Origins of Shame

1. Donald Nathanson, *Shame and Pride: Affect, Sex and the Birth of the Self* (New York: Norton, 1992), p. 11.

2. ibid., p. 52.

3. S. Tomkins, *Affect/imagery/consciousness, Vol. 2: The Negative Affects*, (New York: Springer, 1963). Quoted in Nathanson, *Shame and Pride,*. p. 146.

4. H. Kohut, *The Analysis of the Self* (Madison: International Universities Press, 1971).

5. P. Mollon, *The Fragile Self: The Structure of Narcissistic Disturbance* (London: Whurr Publishers, 1993).

6. ibid., p. 65.

7. Rowan Williams, *Lost Icons* (Edinburgh: T. & T. Clark, 2000), pp. 98–9.

8. Shakespeare, *King Lear*, Arden Edition (London: Methuen, 1964), Act I, Sc. iv.

9. ibid, Act II, Sc. iv.

10. M. Pines, 'The Universality of Shame: A Psychoanalytic Approach', *British Journal of Psychotherapy* Vol. 11(3) (1995), p. 348.

11. T. Scheff, *Emotions, the Social Bond, and Human Reality* (Cambridge University Press, 1997).

12. S. Pattison, *Shame: Theory, Therapy and Theology* (Cambridge University Press, 2000).

13. William Wordsworth, *The Prelude, Book 1*, 1805 (Harmondsworth: Penguin, 1971), p. 56.

4. Shame and Postmodern Culture

1. Rowan Williams, *Lost Icons* (Edinburgh: T. & T. Clark, 2000), pp. 95–138.

2. ibid., p. 102.

3. Pete Ward, *Youthwork and the Mission of God* (London: SPCK, 1997).

4. Amongst the earliest proponents of the idea of 'ordinary' culture were the British socialist commentators Raymond Williams (*Culture and Society*, Chatto and Windus, 1958) and E. P. Thompson (*The Making of the English Working Class*, Victor Gollancz, 1963). Here popular culture is contrasted with 'high culture' and the traditional culture of the working

class contrasted with 'mass media' culture derived from the United States.

5. Stuart Hall and Tony Jefferson, *Resistance through Rituals* (London: Hutchinson, 1975), pp. 5ff.
6. Tom Kitwood, *Dementia Reconsidered*, (Buckingham: Open University Press, 1997), cited in S. Pattison, *Shame: Theory, Therapy and Theology* (Cambridge University Press, 2000), p. 175.
7. Jonathan Sacks, '"Spirituality" is escapist, shallow and self-indulgent', *The Times*, Saturday 24 August 2002.
8. ibid.
9. Williams, *Lost Icons*, pp. 22–3.
10. James W. Fowler, *Faithful Change* (Nashville: Abingdon Press, 1996), p. 12.
11. ibid., pp. 114–31.
12. ibid., p. 122.
13. Christopher Lasch, *The Culture of Narcissism: American Life in an Age of Diminishing Expectations* (New York: Norton, 1979), p. 7.
14. ibid., p.42, quoting Michael Beldoch, 'The Therapeutic as Narcissist', *Salmagundi* 20 (1972), pp. 136, 138.

5. Shame and Sex

1. Rowan Williams, 'Forbidden Fruit' in Martyn Percy (ed.), *Intimate Affairs* (London: Darton, Longman and Todd, 1997), p. 25.
2. Angela Tilby, 'When Harry Met Sally' in Percy (ed.), *Intimate Affairs*, pp. 42–51.
3. Janet Morley, *All Desires Known* (London: SPCK, 1992), p. 113.
4. Augustine, *City of God*, XXII.17, trs. Henry Bettenson (Harmondsworth: Penguin, 1972), p. 1057.
5. Rowan Williams, 'The Body's Grace' in Eugene F. Rogers Jr (ed.), *Theology and Sexuality: Classic and Contemporary Readings* (Oxford: Blackwell, 2002), p. 312.
6. ibid.

6. Shame and Depression

1. B. Andrews, 'Shame and childhood abuse' in P. Gilbert and B. Andrews (eds), *Shame: Interpersonal Behaviour, Psychopathology and Culture* (New York: Oxford University Press, 1998), pp. 176–90.
2. P. Mollon, *The Fragile Self: The Structure of Narcissistic Disturbance* (London: Whurr Publishers, 1993), p. 50.
3. W. P. Sacco and A. T. Beck, 'Cognitive theory and therapy' in E. E. Beckham and W. R. Leber (eds), *Handbook of Depression*, 2nd edn (New York: Guildford Press, 1995), pp. 329–51.

4. P. Gilbert, *Counselling for Depression*, 2nd edn (London: Sage, 2000), pp. 51–75.
5. W. Dryden, 'The use of chaining in rational-emotive therapy', *Journal of Rational-Emotive Therapy* 7 (1989), 59–66.
6. Gilbert, *Counselling for Depression*, p. 167.
7. ibid., pp. 170–1.
8. ibid., p. 172.
9. ibid., p. 174.

7. Jesus and Shame

1. I am indebted here to Kenneth Bailey's literary-cultural interpretation of the parables. Cf. *Poet and Peasant* (Grand Rapids: Eerdmans, 1976), ch. 7 for a detailed exegesis of Luke 15.

8. Shame: A Cure?

1. S. Pattison, *Shame: Theory, Therapy and Theology* (Cambridge University Press, 2000), pp. 170–180.
2. ibid., p. 156.
3. John Bradshaw, *Healing the Shame that Binds You* (Deerfield Beach, Florida: Health Communications Inc., 1988).

9. Shame and the Face

1. Ted Hughes, *Tales from Ovid* (London: Faber and Faber, 1997), pp. 74–84.
2. P. Mollon, *The Fragile Self: The Structure of Narcissistic Disturbance* (London: Whurr Publishers, 1993), pp. 33–5.
3. B. Amsterdam and M. Levitt, 'Consciousness of self and painful self-consciousness', *Psychoanalytical Study of the Child* 35, pp. 67–83, cited in Mollon, *The Fragile Self*.
4. L. Wurmser, *The Mask of Shame* (Baltimore, Maryland: Johns Hopkins University Press, 1981).
5. David Ford, *Self and Salvation: Being Transformed* (Cambridge University Press, 1999), p. 172.
6. James W. Fowler, *Faithful Change* (Nashville: Abingdon Press, 1996), p. 90.
7. S. Pattison, *Shame: Theory, Therapy and Theology* (Cambridge University Press, 2000), p. 229.
8. N. T. Wright, '$\alpha\rho\pi\alpha\gamma\mu\sigma\varsigma$ and the Meaning of Philippians 2:5–11', *Journal of Theological Studies* NS Vol. 37, Pt 2 (October 1986), pp. 321–52; C. F. D. Moule, 'Further Reflection on Philippians 2:5–11' in W. Ward Gasque and Ralph D. Martin (eds), *Apostolic History and the Gospel* (Carlisle: Paternoster Press, 1970), pp. 264–76; C. A. Wanamaker, 'Philippians

2:6–11: Son of God or Adamic Christology?', *New Testament Studies* Vol. 33 (1987), pp. 179–93.

9. Pattison, *Shame: Theory, Therapy and Theology,* pp. 236–41, quote p. 241.

10. Paul Goodliff, *Care in a Confused Climate: Pastoral Care and Postmodern Culture* (London: Darton, Longman and Todd, 1998), pp. 147–58.

10. Mirrored Glory: A Biblical Exploration

1. W. C. van Unnik,'"With Unveiled Face", an Exegesis of 2 Corinthians iii 12–18', *Novum Testamentum* 6 (1963), 153–69; J. D. G. Dunn, '2 Corinthians III. 17 – "The Lord is the Spirit"', *JTS NS* 21 (1970), 309–20; N, T. Wright, 'Reflected Glory: 2 Corinthians 3:18' in I. D. Hurst and N. T. Wright (eds), *The Glory of Christ in the New Testament* (Oxford: Clarendon Press, 1987), pp. 139–150; Richard B. Hays, *Echoes of Scripture in the Letters of Paul* (New Haven: Yale University Press, 1989), Ch. 4; Ralph P. Martin, *2 Corinthians Word Biblical Commentary*, (Waco: Word, 1986), pp. 43–74.

2. Wright, *The Glory of Christ in the New Testament*, p. 140.

3. Hays, *Echoes of Scripture in the Letters of Paul*, p. 133.

4. ibid., p. 137.

5. Wright, *The Glory of Christ in the New Testament*, p. 145.

12. Pastoral Practice in Reducing and Averting Shame

1. Paul Goodliff, *Care in a Confused Climate: Pastoral Care and Postmodern Culture* (London: Darton, Longman and Todd, 1998), pp. 129–35.

2. Christopher Perry, *Listen to the Voice Within* (London: SPCK, 1991).

3. ibid., p. 18.

4. S. Pattison, *Shame: Theory, Therapy and Theology* (Cambridge University Press, 2000), p. 279.

5. ibid., p. 280.

6. Colin Gunton, *The One, the Three and the Many: God, Creation and the Culture of Modernity*, The 1992 Bampton Lectures (Cambridge University Press, 1993), p. 75.

7. Augustine, *Confessions* XI, 14.

8. Alan J. Torrance, 'The Self-Relation, Narcissism and the Gospel of Grace', *Scottish Journal of Theology* Vol. 40 (1987), pp. 481–510, p. 497.

9. ibid., p. 501.

BIBLIOGRAPHY

➤◄

Amsterdam, B. and Levitt, M., 'Consciousness of self and painful self-consciousness', *Psychoanalytical Study of the Child* 35 (1980), pp. 67–83

Andrews, B., 'Shame and childhood abuse' in P. Gilbert and B. Andrews (eds) *Shame: Interpersonal Behaviour, Psychopathology and Culture* (New York: Oxford University Press, 1998), pp. 176–90

Atkinson, D., *The Message of Ruth: The Wings of Refuge* (Leicester: InterVarsity Press, 1983)

Augustine, *City of God*, trs. Henry Bettenson (Harmondsworth: Penguin, 1972)

Bailey, K., *Poet and Peasant* (Grand Rapids: Eerdmans, 1976)

Beldoch, M., 'The Therapeutic as Narcissist', *Salmagundi* 20 (1972)

Bradshaw, J., *Healing the Shame that Binds You* (Deerfield Beach, Florida: Health Communications Inc., 1988)

Dowrick, S., *Forgiveness and Other Acts of Love* (London: The Women's Press, 1997)

Dryden, W., 'The use of chaining in rational-emotive therapy', *Journal of Rational-Emotive Therapy* 7 (1989), pp. 59–66

Dunn, J. D. G., '2 Corinthians III.17 – "The Lord is the Spirit"', *JTS NS* 21 (1970), pp. 309–20.

Ford, D., *Self and Salvation: Being Transformed* (Cambridge University Press, 1999)

Fowler, J. T., *Faithful Change* (Nashville: Abingdon Press, 1996)

Gilbert, P., *Counselling for Depression*, 2nd edn (London: Sage, 2000)

Goodliff, P., *Care in a Confused Climate: Pastoral Care and Postmodern Culture* (London: Darton, Longman and Todd, 1998)

Gunton , C., *The One, the Three and the Many: God, Creation and the Culture of Modernity*, The 1992 Bampton Lectures (Cambridge University Press, 1993)

Hall, S. and Jefferson, T., *Resistance through Rituals* (London: Hutchinson, 1975)

Hays, R. B., *Echoes of Scripture in the Letters of Paul* (New Haven: Yale University Press, 1989)

Hughes, T., *Tales from Ovid* (London: Faber and Faber, 1997)

Jacoby, M., *Shame and the Origins of Self-esteem: A Jungian Approach* (London: Routledge, 1994)

Kitwood, T., *Dementia Reconsidered* (Buckingham: Open University Press, 1997)

Kohut, H., *The Analysis of the Self* (Madison: International Universities Press, 1971)

Lasch, C., *The Culture of Narcissism: American Life in an Age of Diminishing Expectations* (New York: Norton, 1979)

Martin, R. P., *2 Corinthians: Word Biblical Commentary* (Waco: Word, 1986)

Mollon, P., *The Fragile Self: The Structure of Narcissistic Disturbance* (London: Whurr Publishers, 1993)

Morley , J., *All Desires Known* (London: SPCK, 1992)

Moule, C. F. D., 'Further Reflections on Philippians 2:5–11' in W. Ward Gasque and Ralph D. Martin (eds), *Apostolic History and the Gospel* (Carlisle: Paternoster Press, 1970), pp. 264–76

Nathanson, D., *The Many Faces of Shame* (New York: Guildford Press, 1987)

—*Shame and Pride: Affect, Sex, and the Birth of the Self* (NewYork: Norton, 1992)

Pattison, S., *Shame: Theory, Therapy and Theology* (Cambridge: Cambridge University Press, 2000)

Perry, C., *Listen to the Voice Within* (London: SPCK, 1991)

Pines, M., 'The Universality of Shame: A Psychoanalytic Approach', *British Journal of Psychotherapy* Vol. 11(3) (1995)

Sacco, W. P. and Beck, A. T., 'Cognitive theory and therapy' in E. E. Beckham and W. R. Leber (eds), *Handbook of Depression*, 2nd edn (New York: Guildford Press, 1995), pp. 329–51

Sacks, J., '"Spirituality" is escapist, shallow and self-indulgent', *The Times*, Saturday 24 August 2002

Scheff, T., *Emotions, the Social Bond, and Human Reality* (Cambridge: Cambridge University Press, 1997)

Schneider, C. D., 'Shame' in Rodney J. Hunter (ed.) *Dictionary of Pastoral Care and Counselling* (Nashville: Abingdon Press, 1990), pp. 1160–3

Shakespeare, *King Lear*, Arden Edition (London: Methuen, 1964)

Stockitt, R., '"Love Bade Me Welcome; But My Soul Drew Back" – Towards an Understanding of Shame', *Anvil* Vol. 15(2) (1998), pp. 111–119

Thompson, E. P., *The Making of the English Working Class* (London: Victor Gollancz, 1963)

Tilby, A., 'When Harry Met Sally' in Martyn Percy (ed.), *Intimate Affairs* (London: Darton, Longman and Todd, 1997), pp. 42–51

Tomkins, S., *Affect/imagery/consciousness Vol 2: The Negative Affects* (New York: Springer, 1963)

Torrance, A. J., 'The Self-Relation, Narcissism and the Gospel of Grace', *Scottish Journal of Theology* Vol. 40 (1987), pp. 481–510 van Unnik, W. C., '"With Unveiled Face", an Exegesis of 2 Corinthians iii 12–18', *Novum Testamentum* 6 (1963), pp. 153–69

Wanamaker, C. A., 'Philippians 2:6–11: Son of God or Adamic Christology?', *New Testament Studies* Vol. 33 (1987), pp. 179–193

Ward, P., *Youthwork and the Mission of God* (London: SPCK, 1997)

Williams, Raymond, *Culture and Society* (London: Chatto and Windus, 1958)

Williams, Rowan, 'Forbidden Fruit' in Martyn Percy (ed.), *Intimate Affairs* (London, Darton, Longman and Todd, 1997)

—*Lost Icons* (Edinburgh: T. & T. Clark, 2000)

—'The Body's Grace' in Eugene F. Rogers Jr (ed.), *Theology and Sexuality: Classic and Contemporary Readings* (Oxford: Blackwell, 2002)

Wordsworth, W., *The Prelude, Book 1*, 1805 (Harmondsworth: Penguin, 1971)

Wright, N. T., 'αρπαγμος and the Meaning of Philippians 2:5–11', *Journal of Theological Studies* NS Vol. 37, Pt 2 (October 1986), pp. 321–352

—'Reflected Glory: 2 Corinthians 3:18' in I. D. Hurst and N. T. Wright (eds), *The Glory of Christ in the New Testament* (Oxford: Clarendon Press, 1987), pp. 139–150

Wurmser, L., *The Mask of Shame* (Baltimore: Johns Hopkins University Press, 1981)

INDEX OF SCRIPTURE REFERENCES

INDEX OF AUTHORS

GENERAL INDEX

➜❮